July 12.

Moral philos

THE VALUE OF LIFE

(From a Positivist standpoint)

A REPLY TO

MR. MALLOCK'S ESSAY

"IS LIFE WORTH LIVING?"

By

Dr. Mary Putnam Jacobi

" Toute question philosophique et morale finira, selon nous, par apparaitre comme une question sociale."
—*Fouillée*, *Revue des Deux Mondes*, 15 *Juillet*, 1879

NEW YORK
G. P. PUTNAM'S SONS
182 FIFTH AVENUE
1879

IS LIFE WORTH LIVING?

A REPLY.

I.

IF we might be permitted to compare small things with great, we would like to compare Mr. Mallock with the Emperor Julian.

Pause! mighty shade! and avert thy impending wrath at this fancied belittlement of thy just renown, while we explain our not disrespectful meaning.

We mean that if this present age be as truly an eclipse of faith as Mr. Mallock affirms,—an eclipse of the Christian faith, dominant for fifteen centuries,—it can be compared with no epoch which has preceded it so much as with the fourth century of the Christian era. Then also a faith dating from more than fifteen centuries had been undermined,—and was threatened with speedy dissolution,—when a final, a supreme effort was made to reinstate it in its old place,—when a man appeared, hardy enough to try to reverse the irrevocable decrees of destiny: to revive the ancient faith,—to set up again old gods on their mutilated pedestals. The failure of this supreme effort was so complete, that, as every one knows, this champion of the elder gods became branded as an apostate by the victorious disciples of the new,—and hard has it been to rescue his memory from the calumnies which have been heaped upon it. It would of course be premature to attribute a similar failure to the heroic efforts of Mr. Mallock: it would be cruel to suspect that the halo of calumny would ever encircle his memory. But it is permitted to see that in purpose, in desire, and above all in attitude towards the ideas and forces tending to prevail in their respective generations, the Roman emperor and the English essayist have very much in common.

Two strong bases of argument are common to both: the recollection of the glories of the past, and the forecast of the dangers of the future. Every powerful past must have had powers entitling it to respect, and every living future is awaited by dangers, since danger is inseparable from living. At the present day no one denies the power of either Greek polytheism or of mediæval Catholicism. But in regard to the dangers of Catholicism, which were or might have been foreseen by Julian, and to those of Positivism, so vividly apprehended by Mr. Mallock, there is a very wide difference of opinion. As a rule, those who would agree with him that Positivism threatens to enwrap the world at night, or at least twilight, are disposed to regard the rise of Catholicism as the dawn of day.

It would be incorrect however, to reverse the proposition and say that all those who look upon Positivism as the only means of rescuing the European world from intellectual and moral anarchy, were disposed to look upon Catholic Christianity as a delirious episode in the history of Europe. It is well known that Comte himself entertained the profoundest veneration for Catholicism, as a perfect, an admirable type of the régime which it was his mission to inaugurate for the final state of humanity. He even denounced Julian, and associated him with the first Napoleon in a common condemnation, as the two great reactionists of the Christian era; "of whom the first was the most insensate, and the last the most criminal." This opinion was the consequence of the strong conviction held by Comte, that it was the unification of faith and of social life effected by the Catholic church, which first rendered possible the Positivist conception, by which humanity was unified into a living organism. On this account he constantly maintained, that humanity owed a never ceasing debt of gratitude to the Catholic church; and that the new social polity could only be successfully elaborated by pouring its spirit into the exact forms left vacant by the destruction of the spirit of ecclesiasticism. Thus Comte, by a singular turn of thought which afterwards deepened into a settled perversity, would have been the last to recognize any real evil in the triumph of Catholicism,—such as could in any way have justified Julian's struggle to avert this. On the other hand, his disciples, who have developed many of his fundamental principles in full liberty of criticism, have generally been impatient of this detailed comparison between Positivism and Catholicism, and have thought that the latter, "minus Christianity," was less tolerable than when it expressed all the Christain dogma.

This is probably why Mr. Mallock asserts that Prof. Huxley, "one of the most vigorous of our Positivist writers, is a trenchant and contemptuous critic of Positivism in the narrower sense." It is Positivists of this stamp who can see most clearly the real evils inherent in the nature of the Catholic system; who, after enumerating the crimes and misery which, not as mere accidents, but as logical consequences of its fundamental principles, marked the complete triumph of Catholicism, would be prepared to justify a resistance to its ascendency, even more energetic than that offered by Julian, and who yet are convinced that this ascendency was absolutely necessary for the destruction of evils, more ultimately fatal to society than those which succeeded them. When the world had run riot from excess of life unchecked by any real knowledge, when rank and poisonous growths had everywhere stifled wholesome fruit, until the entire empire seemed changed into a vast morass, at once luxuriant and barren, at such a time it is scarcely possible to imagine a more powerful influence for good than that derived from the forcible wrenching away from earth of supreme desires, hopes and ambitions, in order to attach them to a vision of heaven. Difficult to imagine how otherwise the world could have been saved. Easy to see moreover, that this vision would have remained sterile of results, had it not been able to attract the sensuous elements it combated by rewards innately affiliated to their own nature. The sensuousness everywhere inherent in Catholicism, in its doctrine, its discipline, its polity, was essential to the success of its great primitive mission, the conquest of social sensuality.*

Real Catholics, like Mr. Mallock, can never forget that this was the primitive mission of the church; and correlatively can never cease to believe that any relaxation of her influence must immediately be followed by a revival of "the buried lusts of paganism."† Real Positivists, however, never forget the truth embodied in the proverb, "Circumstances alter cases;" never forget that the fulfilment of a mission is in itself the surest portent of the decay of a power; and believe themselves able to demonstrate such a radical change in the conditions of things since the period of the inauguration of Christianity,—that the clearest foreboding of evil to come would no more suggest recourse to ancient methods of salvation, than would the surest provisions of war suggest to a modern city the precaution of laying in a stock of catapults and battering rams. Such persons may listen with

* And to which we believe the mission of "social unification," important though it be, was secondary.

† We quote Mr. Mallock's own expressions, and shall have abundant occasion to refer to his constant preoccupation on this point.

all patience to the Julians of the day, to those who attempt to stem the rising tides on account of the garbage which its waves strew upon the sea shore. They may preserve a respectful consideration for those whose opposition to new things is dictated by a sincere horror of the new forms of evil brought in their train; for those who from the circumstances of their position are unable to perceive the real drift of the current, or to estimate the real strength of the forces which are sweeping it onward. Their courtesy however, will not fail to be much shorter lived towards those whose fears shall prove to have been affected, or whose mental limitations shall appear to have been consciously maintained. And in this connection we cannot but remember—notwithstanding our own desire to accord to Mr. Mallock all the benefit of every doubt, and even the full share of honorable respect now, so tardily paid to Julian; we cannot, we say, conceal from ourselves that all our contemporaries are not equally courteous. Thus, his colleagues in the *Nineteenth Century* do sometimes castigate him severely—not for religious or philosophical reactionism, but for wilful coarsness in his interpretation of contemporary artists.* And a still more recent but anonymous contributor to the *Atlantic Monthly*, has not hesitated to define our author, not as the heroic champion of a failing faith, but simply as "a gentleman who spends

---

* See *Nineteenth Century*, 1878, criticism of Mr. Mallock's criticism of Burne-Jones and Alma Tadema in the preceding number of the Review.

a good deal of his time in defaming his betters.*

The manner in which Mr. Mallock sets forth his apprehensions remind us somewhat of those very pictures that he has criticised so savagely, and in which the clearness of the outline is a good deal sacrificed to the brilliancy of the color. The following passage is indeed a quotation, and from some unknown writer; but our author has endorsed it in such a manner as to make it his own :—

" Never in the history of man has so terrific a calamity befallen the race as that which all who look may now behold,—advancing as a deluge, black with destruction, resistless in might, uprooting our most cherished hopes, engulfing our most precious creed, and burying our highest life in mindless desolation."

If this passage be not sublime, it certainly is for no lack of the vagueness of sublimity. It is however, the ungracious task of a reviewer to endeavor to dispel vagueness by means of interpretation. Like St. Paul, at the very moment of pointing out a "mystery" or "hidden thing," he is compelled to reveal it, and if possible to make it plain. As in justice bound, we will try to make Mr. Mallock's meaning plain, first by means of the definitions of it contained in his own book.

" What I am about to deal with in this book," he says, " is a question which may well strike many, at first sight, as a question that has no serious meaning, or none at any

---

* *Atlantic Monthly*, August, 1879, p. 255.

rate for the sane and healthy mind. I am about to attempt inquiring, not sentimentally, but with all calmness and sobriety, into the true value of this human life of ours, as tried by those tests of reality which the modern world is accepting, and to ask dispassionately if it be really worth the living. The inquiry certainly has often been made before; but it has never been made properly; it has never been made in the true scientific spirit. It has always been vitiated either by diffidence or by personal feeling; and the positive school, though they rejoice to question everything else, have at least in this country left the worth of life alone.* They may now and then perhaps, have affected to examine it; but their examination has been merely formal, like that of a custom-house officer, who passes a portmanteau which he has only opened. They have been as tender with it as Don Quixote was with his mended helmet, when he would not put his card-paper vizor to the test of the steel sword. I propose to supply this deficiency in their investigations. I propose to apply exact thought to the only great subject to which it has not been applied already." (pp. 1 and 2.)

Mr. Mallock then proceeds to explain that by this question, he does not mean "the old ejaculation of satiety or despair, as old as human nature itself;" nor does he mean the question whether the "balance of life's pain is

* This limitation apparently refers to the pessimistic school in Germany, of Schopenhauer and Hartmann,—a school which certainly has little resemblance to Positivism.

necessarily and always in excess of its pleasures." What he proposes to discuss is, "not the superfluous truism that life has been found worth living by many; but the profoundly different proposition that it ought to be found worth living by all." "The meaning of the epithets frequently bestowed on life, (sacred, solemn, earnest, significant, etc.), are that life has some deep inherent world of its own, beyond what it can acquire or lose by the caprice of circumstances, a world, which though it may be most fully revealed to a man through certain forms of success, is yet not destroyed or made a minus quantity by failure." "Does the general reverence with which life is at present regarded, (even by the Positivists) rest upon a misconception?" (Such as the author attributes to Miss Martineau, in having "a grotesque over-estimate of her own social and intellectual importance.")

Mr. Mallock argues that the belief in life may easily be one day destroyed, because "the belief in God, and in a supernatural order, once supposed to rest on an equally wide basis, has in these days not been questioned only, but has to a great degree been successfully annihilated." "The emotion of reverence towards life will not go further towards proving that it deserves reverence, than does the fact that men loved God and felt his presence close to them, prove to the positive thinker, God's existence." (p. 8.)

Mr. Mallock asserts that in modern times, the import of the question, "Is life worth living?" has entirely changed. Formerly when men commented on the mysteries of life, they consoled themselves by a hope of the future,—"of spiritual and eternal destinies; they remembered that there were triumphs beyond all hope, and portentous failures beyond all fear." But the modern Positivists and their work cannot be compared even with the "infidels" of antiquity. "The denial which is spreading itself over the world is far more complete than ever before; and moreover, into both it and the correlative assertion enter certain factors which at once make such comparisons worthless." These factors are, the existence of Christianity, the change in the conception of the world, and the development of an intense social self-consciousness. The influence of Christianity depends upon the clearness into which it has "focalised light of the supernatural," so that the conception of this possesses a power hitherto unknown, and upon the increased sense of human dignity which has resulted from its views of the relations between God and man.

The difficulty about the world is, simply, that it has grown practically smaller, because people find it a great deal easier to travel round it. Hence it offers far fewer resources to the imagination, and all happiness depending upon this is by so much diminished. At the very time that Positivism is making greater demands upon the earth for human happiness, the earth is becoming less able to meet them.

Finally, civilized man has become so self-conscious that

he has lost much of his old spontaneity of action; he will admit nothing without question, take to pieces all motives, and, so far as he is influenced by positive thought, reduces all religions to ideals created by his own intelligence.

These three facts, or "factors," as Mr. Mallock calls them rather ambiguously, and whose details we shall consider later, so change the modern horizon—that modern and antique thought cannot really resemble each other, even when apparently tending in the same direction. The great danger is that this new and "damning self-consciousness" may "contain a negation of the supernatural." A negation in the consciousness of Lucretius would be of little importance; he had not known Christianity, and sinned, therefore, with his eyes shut. But for those to whom the Gospel has been preached, the matter is very different; they sin or deny with their eyes open; and if the negation be sustained, it is "impossible but what humanity will one day find itself in the position of a man who awakes from a dream, and finds all that he most prized vanished from him," for such an awakening will be a sort of "discovery of man by himself," which "will then certainly be the beginning of his decadence; he will find himself to be a lesser and a lower thing than he thought he was, and his condition must continue to sink till it tallies with his own conception of it." (p. 199.)

"The path of thought, as it were, has taken a sudden turn round a mountain, and our bewildered eyes are staring in undreamed-of prospect. The leaders of progress thus far have greeted the sight with acclamation, and have confidently declared that we are looking on the promised land. But to the more thoughtful and less impulsive it is plain that a mist hangs over it, and that we have no right to be sure whether it is the promised land or no. They see grave reasons for making a closer scrutiny, and for asking if, when the mist lifts, what we see will be not splendor, but desolation."

This is the new import of the "momentous question," into which Mr. Mallock, like the traditional spider, invites the unwary public to walk into his little parlor of labyrinthine discussion. The labyrinth is not in itself either grim or displeasing: its devious ways appear, at least at first sight, as elegant as those of Rosamond's bower, while the walls are so low and easily surmounted, that anyone who gets tired of strolling along in the regular line of argument, can vault over them in a twinkling and find himself at once in free air. The argument is all the better adapted to popular reading, that it is derived exclusively from discussion of popular essays, and reads like one of those drawing-room after-dinner talks of which Mr. Mallock is so fond. He seems more anxious to keep near to the heart of his audience than of his subject, and, perhaps, on this account, avoids grappling with this subject as it is set forth in systematic treatises, and by the founders of doctrine, and only closes with it as presented in light armor, in popular essays and reviews. We find in Mr. Mallock's book no mention of Comte, nor Littré nor Spencer, nor Lewes, nor Bain, nor Darwin, nor Haeckel. His presentations of philosophy are obtained from naturalists, as Huxley and Clifford, or from romance writers, as George Eliot and Theophile Gautier. His illustrations of physiology are quoted from the physicist, Tyndall, and for psychology, he quotes no authority at all. Yet if ever theme could be considered psychological, a question on the estimate of life, to be made by the persons enjoying it, would certainly seem to be one.

Having stated the question in the terms above quoted, Mr. Mallock proceeds to discuss the "claim for life as made by the positive school themselves." * At the outset he discards the idea that life can possess any intrinsic worth; he answers, as a matter on which all are agreed, that its significance depends on some "Prize," definite and unique, possibly obtainable by its energies. The real question at issue with the Positivists is, "What is the nature of this Prize? How does their definition of it correspond with that given by other people?" Again, it is assumed as a universally conceded truth, accepted by Positivists as well as by Transcendentalists, that this Prize, or the "worth of life, is closely bound up with what we call morality," and the specific difference to be found in Positivist views depends upon their special explanation

* This error of grammar is not ours; it lies between the author and the printer.

of what this supremacy of morality means. Another special character depends on the fact that the Positivists admit the existence of no life for human beings other than that which is visibly passed in this world. This Prize, therefore, whatever it is, must be obtained or obtainable by "flesh and blood creatures," by man before he dies, and during his common daily life. While the Catholic, on the contrary, has all eternity to choose from, and the smaller the prospect of prizes here, the greater the probability of drawing an ineffable prize hereafter.

Narrowing down the definitions, Mr. Mallock decides, by means of two or three quotations from "Positivist" writers, that this "Prize" is some "form of happiness," which must, therefore, be susceptible of exact description. Since the Positivists are always insisting upon the possibility of "mental presentation," Mr. Mallock considers it but just that they be expected to give a definite picture of this earthly paradise which they propose to substitute for all the Christian hopes of heaven. This is what he calls "applying exact thought."

But impartial scrutiny of the descriptions of this happiness shows that it is at least as vague as the most mystical vision of the saints, and that its attributes are inconsistent with each other. They correspond neither to any internal pattern of what they are said to be, nor to any external model of what we could justly expect them to be. They are not distinct nor "mentally presentable;" they are not even visible to more than a limited part of the world; they are not capable of being made attractive to any one who does not naturally admire them,—hence, even when confirming the virtuous in his appreciation of virtue, they are useless as a means of convincing the vicious of the folly of vice. At this point our author, who has hitherto spoken of the Prize of Life only as being something "closely bound up with morality," now *identifies* it with morality itself, and clinches his demonstration of the futility of the Positivist's conception of happiness, with the remark: "It is clear that if a morality is incapable of being preached, it is useless to say that it is worthy of being practised."

The identification once made is continued throughout the remainder of the discussion. Nowhere do we find any attempt to formally distinguish between "happiness" and "morality," although at the outset, even in asserting their close connection, the author acknowledges by implication that they are distinct.

Mr. Mallock does not attempt to define the nature of "morality," according either to a conception of his own or of Positivism. Instead of this, he offers a definition of a code of morals. It consists of a number of restraining orders; it rigorously bids us walk in certain paths, in preference to a number of other paths in which we are naturally inclined to walk. "The law has arisen because of transgression, and the moralist has to meddle with human nature mainly because it is inconstant and corrupted."

In all this it is assumed that the Positivists and Catholics cannot fail to agree. "*Positive* morality" only differs from any other kind (as far as we may judge from the exposition of our author,) by "presupposing that life by its very nature contains the possibility in it of some one kind of happiness which is open to all men, and which is better than all others. The proudest, the serenest, the most successful life of vice, must be miserable when compared with the most painful life of virtue, and miserable in a very high degree; for morality is momentous exactly in proportion to the interval between the things to be gained and escaped by it." (p. 44.)

Mr. Mallock is not anxious that what the Positivists may mean by the Prize of Life, should be made clear. But it is noteworthy that he terminates his chapter on this subject without making it at all clear what he himself would mean in contradistinction to them. It is only by implication that we may infer the difference to principally consist in this: that the Positivists expect to obtain the prizes of life in this world or not at all; while the Catholic Christian professes to believe that nothing in this life is really worth having, but that prizes of untold magnitude are to be obtained after death, during a future life, to be sustained in another locality. It is this conviction to which Mr. Emerson refers when he says, "We are to have just *such* a good time in the next world as the wicked have in this." The alleged "spirituality" of the Christian hope depends largely on the simple fact that it is a hope deferred. The "materialism" of the Positivist enjoyments is seen from the fact that they are obtained by persons yet "clothed upon with flesh and blood." "This is the great question," insists Mr. Mallock: "Is such happiness a reality or a myth? Can human life, cut off utterly from every hope beyond itself, supply it?" (p. 44.)

Still oscillating backwards and forwards between morality and happiness—whose connection together he has not yet defined—Mr. Mallock complains that the Positivists oscillate incessantly between definition of personal and of social happiness, which mutually confuse each other so that it is impossible to tell which they really hold to be the crowning achievement of life. Their speculations on happiness are, however, all vitiated "by a subtle but profound defect; they constantly confuse the negative condition of happiness with the positive materials of it." Returning then, without line of demarkation to the question of morality, Mr. Mallock tells us that, according to the theory of utilitarianism, "morals possess a positive basis in the acknowledged science of sociology." We are told further that the "province of the sociologist is the study of human action as productive or non-productive of some certain general good. Inasmuch, however, as Positivists cannot be made to define in an intelligible manner what this general good is, the difficulty of understanding morals by means of sociology, becomes as great as that of understanding the Prize of Life by means of either happiness or morals.

According to Mr. Mallock's understanding of the matter, sociology, in the minds of the Positivists, means not so much a science as an art for making everybody comfortable, and the morality of any actions is tested by the degree to which they contribute to this end. The first thing, however, necessary to make people comfortable, is to know what they want, and the trouble is that they are quite as likely to want something very bad as very good. In that case morality must be sacrificed for the sake of the very end which is the basis of morality. Thus, the practice of seduction, sometimes condemned on account of the misery brought by it to its victims and their families, would cease to be so "if the victims were willing and the families complacent, though in the eye of the [Catholic] moralist, matters in this last case will be far worse than in the former." The cultivation of the sympathetic instincts, which is the aim of sociology, and upon which the Positivists rely for the development of the highest virtue, may as easily lead to the meanest vice. For "vice can be enjoyed in common just as well as virtue; nor, if wisely regulated, will it exhaust the tastes that it appeals to. Regulated with equal skill and equal farsightedness, it will take its place side by side with virtue; *nor will sociology or social morality give us any reason for preferring the one to the other*" (p. 57). "Morality, it is true, must rest ultimately on proved facts of sociology;

but it rests upon them as a statue rests upon its pedestal, and the same pedestal will support an Athenè or a Priapus" (p. 59). That is, we persume, that the same facts which can be appealed to in support of a system of morality, can, with equal propriety, be cited in favor of complete immorality, which is certainly a very remarkable and unusual property for facts to possess.

Besides this difficulty, there is another quite as serious, inherent in any system which relies upon the unselfish instincts; they are not strong enough for the purpose. "The general conditions of an entirely undefined happiness form an ideal utterly unfitted to counterbalance individual temptation, or to give even willingness, let alone ardour, to the self-denials that are required of us. In the first place, the conditions are so vague that even in the extremest cases the individual will find it difficult to realize that he is appreciably disturbing them; and, in the second place, until he knows that the happiness in question is something of extreme value, he will be unable to feel much ardor in helping to make it possible" (p. 67). * * * "The first question that the common sense of mankind asks is, 'What shall I get?' and 'You must promise something to each of us, or very certainly you will be able to promise nothing to all of us.' There is no real escape in saying that we must all work for one another, and that our happiness is to be found in that. * * * But what sort of happiness shall I secure for others? and what sort of happiness will others secure for me?"

"The Positivists say," observes Mr. Mallock, "that all mankind are made a mighty whole by the fusing power of benevolence. But happiness must plainly be something besides benevolence, else if I know that a man's highest happiness is in knowing that others are happy, all I shall try to procure for others is the knowledge that I am happy, and thus the Utopian happiness would be expressed completely in the somewhat homely formula, 'I am so glad that you are glad that I am glad.'"

"Many Positivists" (says Mr. Mallock) "attempt to show that goodness is its own reward, and that it is chiefly love which gives to life an incalculable worth." "It will remain a stable possession to us amid the wreck of creeds, and will never fail us as a sure test of conduct. Whatever guides us to this treasure we shall know is moral; whatever tends to withdraw us from it we shall know is immoral." (p. 102.)

But the goodness which the Positivists have in view is something that existed in the world before Positivism came into it, and is mixed with an important element which it is their business to get rid of. This element is religion. "If the beauty of holiness, the love of truth, the treasure of human affection be boiled down, so to speak, until every germ of religion in them is destroyed," it is extremely doubtful whether they would "generate the same ecstatic happiness." (p. 87.)

"There are three principal characteristics of the moral end—its inwardness, its importance, and, within certain limits, its absolute character;" and in all of these "religion is embodied" (p. 88), and for them the theism that modern thought is rejecting, could offer a strictly logical basis." (p. 93.) "But Positivism, although conceiving of the moral end in the same way, sets out from two premises which differ from Theism by consisting of two great denials. These are, there is no personal God, and there is no personal immortality." (p. 96.)

Starting from negative premises, Positivism eliminates two of the characteristics of the moral end, and materially modifies the third. It changes the importance of the moral end "by confining all the life with which we can have the least moral connection to the surface of the earth, to the limited time for which life and consciousness can exist upon it." Thus the moral end has nothing in it whatever of the infinite, and a scientific forecast can already see the end of it.

In the second place it is nothing absolute, and not being absolute, is incapable of being enforced.

In the third place, its value, such as it is, is measured only by the conscious happiness that its possession gives us, or the conscious pain that its loss gives us.

Thus goodness to the Positivist who professes to claim no other reward for goodness than goodness itself, becomes, by his system, deprived of all the qualities by which it might become such a reward. It could only be so to the Theist, who retains those qualities, and who, moreover, in his hope of heaven, possesses other rewards over and above whatever goodness itself may be. In this same incisive (?) manner, Mr. Mallock proceeds to destroy the "incalculable worth" of love for Positivism. Love can be of no elevated utility unless it supplies us with a moral standard; but it can have no moral standard if it be deprived of religious anticipations. "The supposed evils of impurity depend not on any present consciousness, but on the expectations of future consciousness, a consciousness that will reveal things to us hereafter which we can only augur here." (p. 124.) In the absence of this anticipation of future punishment for impurity, all love (so, apparently, is the drift of Mr. Mallock's argument) tends to become impure. "Love as a positive pleasure, if it ever be reduced to such, will be a very different thing from what our Positivist moralists at present see it to be. It will perform none of those functions for which they now look to it. It will no longer supply them as now with any special pinnacle on which human life may raise itself. The one type of it that is at present on an eminence will sink to the same level as the others. All these will be offered to us indiscriminately, and any choice between them will have no moral value."

Thus Mr. Mallock finds frittered away the "resources which have supposed to impart to life a positive general value." (p. 131). "Positivism if accepted fully, must either destroy or paralyze the supernatural moral judgment which has become a primary faculty with us, and which mixes with every estimate we form of the world around us." (p. 133.)

What will then be left in life will not be worth having. All "high art is based upon solemn and profound beliefs in the supernatural, and will disappear with them. The premises on which all its power and greatness rests is this: The grand relation of man is not first to his brother man, but to something else that is beyond humanity, that is at once without and also beyond himself; to this first, and to his brother men through this. We are not ours, we are bought with a price. Our bodies are God's temples, and the joy and the terror of life depends on our keeping these temples pure or defiling them." (p. 139.)

Not only sublime art, but "cynical, profligate and concupiscent art, really appeals to the same motives, but inverted." "The source of the pleasure in one is an impassioned struggle after the supernatural right, or an impassioned sense of rest upon attaining it; the source of the other is the sense of revolt against it, which in various ways flatters or excites us." (p. 43).

"Art without the moral sense to play upon, is like a pianist whose key-board is reduced to a single octave, and life will lose just the same qualities that art will. There will be no introduction of any new interests, but merely the diminution of certain existing ones. The subtraction of the moral sense will not revolutionize human purposes, but merely make them listless. It will reduce to a particolored level the whole field of pains and pleasures. * * * Vice and virtue will be set before us in the same gray light; every deeper feeling either of joy or sorrow, of desire or of repulsion, will lose its vigor, and cease any more to be resonant." (p. 145.)

Mr. Mallock continues to show, or to assert, that even the life of the senses—the joy in the mere act of living, in the exereising of bodily functions, is unconsciously impregnated with a flavor of religion, and by losing this, this joy of living will not indeed "lose existence, but it will lose zest." (p. 147.)

"The last resource of the modern school is devotion to truth." (p. 150). It seems odd to talk of this as a "resource," especially in a school that has just been condemned for destroying "moral judgment," and with it everything that rendered life interesting. Still more strange to find that this "resource" is denied, not as was the case in speaking of goodness and love and art, because Positivism is supposed to have vitiated its value before having recourse to it, but because it is in itself something foolish and absurd. "Truth, as the Positivists speak of it, is plainly a thing to be worshipped in two ways—firstly, by its discovery; secondly, by its publication. Thus Prof. Huxley, however much it may pain him (?), will not hide from himself the fact that there is no God; and however bad this knowledge may be for humanity, his highest and most sacred duty still consists in imparting it." But, according to Mr. Mallock, this is as foolish as it would be for a man to inform another that his wife had been seduced by his best friend, or for a chattering nurse to betray his danger to a sick man, who thereupon takes fright and dies. "Clearly the truth that it is sacred to find out and to publish are not all truths, but truths of a certain kind only. They are not particular truths, but the universal and eternal truths that underlie them. * * * The Theist of course believes that truth is sacred. But his belief rests on a foundation that has been altogether renounced by the Positivist. He values truth because, in whatever direction it takes him, it takes him either to God or towards him. * * * Nature is cruel, wicked and bewildering when ruined by itself. But behind Nature he sees a vaster power—his father—in whom mysteriously all contradictions are reconciled. * * * It is not too much to say that without a religion, without a belief in God, no fetish worship was ever more ridiculous than this cultus of natural truth." (pp. 150–157). And again, "What Professor Huxley's philosophy really proves to him that it is true nothing is sacred; not that it is a sacred thing to discover the truth." (p. 219.)

After a little more consideration of this subject, Mr. Mallock concludes that it is in this last resource of Positivism (*i. e.*, truth,) that religion is embodied as a yet more important element than in any of the others, and when this element is driven out of it, it collapses yet more hopelessly than they do." (p. 161.)

Hence by the positive system, nothing is left in life but life itself, and "it is impossible to conceive of life as being a very valuable possession, even under the most favorable circumstances, with social progress carried to the utmost perfection; and access laid open to every happiness of which man may remain capable."

"The goal to which a purely human progress is capable of conducting us is no more a condition of glory and felicity, in which men shall develop new and ampler powers. It is a condition in which the keenest life attainable has continually been far surpassed already, without anything having been arrived at that in itself seemed of surpassing value." (p. 161.)

Yet the characteristic "superstition of Positivism," is the belief that man's subjective powers of happiness will go on expanding, in the same proportion as the (natural) course of events tends to lessen the imperfections of life, and thus improve its "negative conditions." "It is the belief that existing pleasures will be more diffused, and also that they will grow more intense in diffusion. It is this belief on which the Positivists rely to create that enthusiasm, that impassioned benevolence, which is to be the motive power of their whole ethical machinery." (p. 164.)

According to Mr. Mallock's interpretation, the principle focus of this "impassioned benevolence," is not in the present, but in the future glories of humanity, and he undertakes to demonstrate that these are as vague, as unsatisfactory and as absurd as any Christian heaven can be. "The Positivists ask the Christians how they expect to enjoy themselves in heaven. The Christians may, with far more force, ask the Positivists how they expect to enjoy themselves on earth," and Mr. Mallock proves to his own satisfaction that they will not enjoy themselves at all, or at least that their enjoyments will be so dull and lifeless that they are not worth counting. In the argument upon the intrinsic importance of truth upon which we have already touched, Mr. Mallock distinctly intimates that the truth of a doctrine is always of secondary importance to its attractiveness and to its supposed utility. Thus the two assertions which constantly reappear as arguments in his pages are to the effect, first, this is very tiresome; and second, it is very dangerous. In his chapter on the practical prospect of things as they will be in the event of the triumph of Positivism, these two arguments converge. Thus he discusses the effect of the ruin of conscience which he deems inevitable, in a way that leaves it doubtful whether he is most fearful that the world will lose a police force, or an artistic decoration. "The Positivists find themselves powerless to pass any judgment, or extend the law they live by to any beyond themselves. The whole prospect that environs them has become morally colorless. * * * The authority of conscience cannot survive Positivist analysis, though its voice may.

"The condition of men will be characterized by vain self-reproach, joyless commendation, weary struggle, listless success, general indifference, and the prospect that, if matters are going thus badly with them, they will go even worse with their children." (p. 197.) In a later chapter, returning to the same theme, Mr. Mallock illustrates the moral powerlessness of Positivism by means of an imaginary dialogue held between Dr. Tyndall and "some ruined girl, oppressed with a sense of degradation." "I have heard you are a very wise man," she says to him, "and you have proved that the priest is all wrong, who prepared me a year ago for my confirmation.* Now tell me, I beseech you tell me, is mine really the desperate state I have been taught to think it is? May my body be likened to the temple of the Holy Ghost defiled? or do I owe it no more reverence than I owe the Alhambra Theatre? Am I guilty, and must I seek repentance? or am I not guilty, and may I go on just as I please?"

"My dear girl," Dr. Tyndall replies to her, "I must shake my head in doubt. Come, let us lower our heads and acknowledge our ignorance as to whether you are a wretched girl or not. Materialism is confounded and science rendered dumb by questions such as yours; they can, therefore, never be answered, and must always remain open. I may add, however, that if you ask me

* We think Mr. Mallock might have selected a less precocious example of "ruin" than this must have been then; also one that was less derogatory to the strength of influence of the priest.

personally whether I consider you to be degraded, I lean to the affirmative. But I can give you no reason in support of this judgment, so you may attach to it what value you will."

We confess that this wit seems to us as superficial as that which characterizes the parodies in the "New Republic." But it is not yet time to criticise; we wish to first obtain from Mr. Mallock as complete a statement as possible of his position.

From the considerations which precede, and from which we have omitted nothing essential to the line of argument, Mr. Mallock concludes with great emphasis that "human life will degenerate if the creed of Positivism be ever generally accepted," and that such a degradation has already begun. This is precisely why he comes to the rescue, and tries to open the eyes of his contemporaries to a prospect that becomes the more appalling the more he looks at it. It is true that the present leaders of Positivism are not wicked men, and they will not admit that they are unhappy men. But their integrity is due to their early training in the religion they have discarded; even Mr. Mill, in spite of his protests, having been submitted to a discipline which could be called "Puritanism minus Christianity." And their apparent happiness is but an heroic assumption of cheerfulness that hides an aching void within. They are like soldiers fighting heroically, but with the secret consciousness of a death wound under their armor. Mr. Mallock does not deny that the high moral character of his opponents, lends great weight to their arguments; and expressly asserts that it is to their intellectual prestige, and directly to its own premises, that the power of Positivism is due. "These men, to *the destruction of private judgment, are forcing on us* their own personal conclusions." *

Mr. Mallock admits that the immense victories won by the Positivist method in range of physical science, have created a very strong prejudice in favor of the method, and of its intellectual supremacy.

"The opinion, therefore, that is now abroad in the world is that the positive school *are* [is] the monopolists of unbiassed reason.†" (p. 208.) It is therefore of extreme importance to break down this prestige, and to break up this monopoly, and Mr. Mallock undertakes to do this by attacking what he conceives to be the fundamental principle of the positive philosophy. This is, that, "the entire sensible universe has been brought within the scope of the physicist: that everything that is is matter moving. Life itself is nothing but motion of an infinitely complex kind. It is matter in its finest ferment." "Thus science has unified the apparent dualism of things." "Thought and affections have a certain bulk and a certain place in space, and could conceivably be made the subjects of some physical experiment." "Faith, sanctity, doubt, sorrow and love, could conceivably be all

* The italics are ours.

† Another error of grammar for which we are not responsible.

guaged and detected by some scientific instrument—by a camera or by a spectroscope."

"Thus the achievements of science have taken away any external proof of the existence of God,—and still more, every sign of his daily providence; and again, the life and soul of a man are presented to us, not as an entity distinct from the body and therefore capable of surviving it, but as a function of it, or as the sum of its functions, which has demonstrably grown with its growth, and is dependent upon its minutest changes, and which, for any sign or hint to the contrary, will be dissolved with its dissolution." "A God therefore that is the master of matter, and a human soul that is independent of it, any second world, in fact, of alien and trans-material forces, is reduced on physical grounds, to an utterly unsupported hypothesis," (p. 213)—and the whole force of the foregoing argument (?) rests on the following suppressed premise,—"that nothing exists but what the study of matter could conceivably reveal to us: or that, in other words, the immaterial equals the non-existent."

"There is a great modern axiom, namely, that verification is the test of truth: or that we can build on nothing as certain but what we can prove to be true. * * * A fact is only proved when the evidence it rests upon leaves no room for doubt, when it forces on every mind the same invincible conviction: that is, in other words, *when, directly or indirectly, its material equivalent can be* *impressed upon our bodily senses.** This is the fulcrum of the modern intellectual lever." (p. 214.)

And this is what Mr. Mallock calls "The Logic of Scientific Negation." Formerly when Christians argued with infidels—from Tertullian to Bishop Butler—they entertained no doubt of their ability to demonstrate the truth of their own theme. The proof might be of various kinds, from unimpeachable testimony to conspicuous analogy, but it was always forthcoming. It is not so long since text-books on the "Evidences of Christianity," were entered on the curriculum of the senior class in every well appointed boarding school.

But this time seems to have passed by, and an era to have dawned which may of course prove to be much worse for the "infidels," but in the meantime is certainly much easier and more convenient for the Christians. Under this régime the laborious search for "proof" and "evidence" is abandoned; question of fact and question of analogy are equally laid aside; neither Bridgewater treatise nor Bampton lecture are any further put into requisition, and the admission quickly made, "We *have* no proof." "As to the minor premises, that there is no proof of religion, we may concede, *at least provisionally*, that it is completely true." (p. 215.)

And the rest of Mr. Mallock's essay, is devoted to showing how, though without proof of truth, religion, and the Catholic religion, should, can and must be maintained.

* Italics ours.

The reason for this, therefore, must be outside of the truth of it, and is to be found in the declaration that if "science can take from man his religious faith, it leaves him a being without any moral guidance;" more, "by the same argument it will prove him to be not a moral being at all; that it will prove not only that he has no rule by which to direct his will, but also that he has no will to direct." (p. 220.) "Morality and religion are, so far as science goes on one and the same footing" (p. 243), because they are both immaterial and supernatural, and science, rejecting everything but what is material and natural, has as much reason to reject one as the other, if once allowed to reject either. "Science will allow us to deny or to affirm both," [but not only one]. (p. 246.)

Thus because there is such a thing as morality, and Positivists admit it, and make themselves "ridiculous by applying to it their great test of verification," Mr. Mallock, by means of the above argument, establishes at once that Theism is true, or we should rather say, inevitable, since for Mr. Mallock truth and necessity are not convertible terms. But, with a candor which has become fashionable in similar discussions, Mr. Mallock admits that serious intellectual and moral difficulties stand in the way of acceptance of the doctrine of Theism. Extrication from these difficulties is effected by a judicious exercise of the same ingenuous candor as acknowledged them. They cannot be solved, we are told. They are ways past finding out.* But then these are not the only

* We confess to a hesitation whether the implied reference is more to Job or to Lord Dundreary.

difficulties. Our way is beset with them, and it is easier to accept them all in a lump than to make a pretext of solving some, and then rejecting others because they are insoluble. Thus freedom of the will is a mystery; and the connection between the soul and the body is a mystery; and the relations of the supernatural to the natural are mysteries. Therefore there is no reason that we should reject a belief in God because of the mystery of eternal punishment, or because of the unthinkableness of heaven, or of the difficulty of understanding Providential relations with savages and Bushmen.

This doctrine of equivalent inexplicablenesses, carries Mr. Mallock smoothly through all the classical difficulties of Natural Theism. "If we suppose ourselves once convinced that man will always believe in himself as a moral being, and that he will under no compulsion give up this belief; then it will be plain to us that Theism, should it *ever tend to reassert itself*, can have no check to fear at the *hands* of positive thought." (p. 264) *

Up to this point all the argument of the essay was tended simply towards establishing the probability of Theism, or the at least equal ludicrousness of anything else. But now having reached this somewhat unstable foundation, Mr. Mallock, like a gymnast on a flying trapeze, immediately begins to go up higher. "There is," he says, "no sharp and well defined argument" in favor of the

* The italics are ours, as we cannot help calling attention to the inelegant metaphor on the one hand, and on the other to the unconscious feebleness of the hope expressed in a "revival of faith."

"revival and triumph of any one alleged revelation." Nevertheless the "mass of religious humanity, once possessed of a natural creed,* will be found instinctively and inevitably to ask for more." The only thing a natural creed can do, "is to analyse the worth of life, and of the momentous issues attendant on the way in which they live it," but it is unable to offer any practical guidance. "Natural Theism can tell us with sufficient emphasis that all vice is to be avoided, it is continually at a loss to tell us whether this thing or whether that thing is vicious." (p. 266.) We would notice that this obvious consideration has contributed to render most "Positivists" extremely incredulous in regard to the efficacy of Theism as a consolation and a guide, and thus has led them to reject many promises, such as are made so liberally by Mr. Mallock in the early part of his essay. He tells us at first that belief in God and personal immortality, even when incapable of proof, must nevertheless be strenuously maintained *because* of its immense practical utility. He tells us now that this belief is of no possible practical use unless there be added to it, belief in an infallible revelation.

And as the argument (?) proceeds, the different links are crowded at once more rapidly and more closely together. We are told that "once admitted" the necessity of an infallible revelation, it must be met by one that has

* We cannot help asking how, according to Mr. Mallock's views, a creed about the supernatural, can receive so slighting a designation.

been already made ; and it must be Christian and it must be Catholic, the only branch of the Christian church that has for "primary doctrine her own perpetual infallibility." This doctrine at once establishes the superiority of the church in accordance with a line of argument that is looking not for truth but precisely for infallibility. "Seek, and ye shall find ; knock, and it shall be opened unto you." Mr. Mallock draws an historical sketch exhibiting the development of the church as a "Parliament of the believing world" from the original loose agglomeration of dreamers on spiritual matters or "natural Theists," and tells us (here the links of argument are so closely pressed together that they disappear in a single dogmatic and momentous assertion) "that the church is not only the parliament of spiritual man, but she is such a parliament guided by the spirit of God." (p. 281.) "The analogy of the human brain is here of great help to us. The human brain is an arrangement of material particles which can become connected with consciousness only in virtue of such a special arrangement. The church is theoretically an arrangement of individuals which can become connected with the spirit of God only in virtue of an arrangement equally special ;" *i. e.* as is intimated in the preceding paragraph, the arrangement of "intricate machinery systems of representation, etc."

Mr. Mallock then discusses the "difficulties" of the Catholic dogma, so far he has already discussed the difficulties of natural Theism. On every hand are "mysteries" to be "acknowledged frankly," but not on that account to be "rejected," still less cause "rejection" of the system dependent upon them. There is the mystery that revelation should have been confined to such a small minority of the human race; (p. 282) there is the mystery of Catholic orthodoxy and of Catholic discipline in regard to heretics; (p. 285) there is the mystery of the Eucharist, (p. 287) of the invocation of the saints, of purgatory. (p. 290.) Besides these things, there are many details of discipline, which are not matters of authorized or authoritative faith at all, merely "pious opinions." Such is the rule for celibacy of the clergy; such even, is the temporary belief in the inspiration of the Bible, which, contrary to the Protestant idea, the church has never inculcated as doctrine. "Rigid as were opinions entertained as to Biblical inspiration throughout the greater part of the church's history, the church has never formally assumed them as articles of faith. Had she done so, she might indeed have been convicted of error, for many of these opinions can be shown to be at variance with fact. But though she lived and breathed for so many centuries amongst them, though for ages none of her members perhaps ever doubted their truth, she has not laid them on succeeding ages; she has left them opinions still. A Catholic might well adduce this as an instance, not indeed of her supernatural selection, but of its counterpart, her supernatural rejection." (p. 308.)

"The Catholic church," sums up Mr. Mallock, "is the

only dogmatic religion that has seen what dogmatism really implies, and what will in the long run (!) be demanded of it, and she contains in herself all appliances for meeting these demands. * * * The Catholic church is the only historical religion that can conceivably thus adapt itself to the works of the present day, without virtually ceasing to be itself. * * * All this of course does not prove that Catholicism *is* the truth; *but it will show the Theist, that for all that the modern world can tell him, it may be.*" (p. 313.)*

"The school in question has proceeded from denial to denial, thinking at each successive moment that it had reached its final halting-place, and had struck at last on a solid and firm foundation. First it denied the church to assert the Bible; then it denied the Bible to assert God; then it denied God to assert the moral dignity of man; and there if it could remain it would.

But it is compelled to move onwards; and now, under the force of its own relentless logic, this last resting-place is beginning to fail also. * * * So the battle is to be fought at the very threshold at the entrance to the spiritual world. Are we moral and spiritual beings, or are we not? * * * The decision, if we have a will at all, lies with our own will—with our will alone to make. * * * Can we still resolve to say, "I believe although it is impossible? Is the will to assert our own moral nature, our own birthright in

* Italics ours.

eternity, strong enough to lead us on?" (p. 320.)

If this will can be found, Mr. Mallock assures us with pathos, "everything else will follow." "From his first assent to his own moral nature, man *must* rise to a Theism, and he *may* rise to the recognition of a church—to a visible embodiment of that moral nature of his, as directed and joined to its one aim and end,—to its delight and its desire and its completion. Then he will see all that is high and holy taking a distinct and helping form for him. Grace and mercy will come to him through set and certain channels. His nature will be redeemed visibly from its weakness and from its littleness—redeemed not in dreams or in fancy, but in fact. God himself will be his brother and his father; he will be near akin to the Power that *is* always and *is* everywhere. His love of virtue will be no longer a mere taste of his own; it will be the discernment and taking to himself of the eternal strength and of the eternal treasure; and whatever he most reveres in mother or wife, or sister, this he will know is holy everywhere and forever, and is exalted high over all things in one of like nature with theirs, the Mother of Grace, the Parent of sweet clemency, who will protect him from the enemy and save him in the hour of death." (p. 323.)

And thus, with bowed head and folded hands, Mr. Mallock prostrates himself at the shrine of the Madonna, receiving, in the ecstacy of an ineffable meditation, the heavenly reward of his long and toilsome knight-errantry in this wicked world. And from the confessional near the shrine we seem to hear a sonorous voice issue, crying, "Well done, good and faithful servant! Enter thou into the joy of the church!

II.

We have made this long abstract of Mr. Mallock's essay, in order to set forth his position as far as may be possible in his own words, and thus avoid a misrepresentation. Condensed in a single paragraph, the argument is: Modern science, and Positivism which reposes in it, reduces the entire universe of matter to a mass of physical things. In this mass man is included, and consequently loses all the dignity, interest and pathos which attached to him as a spiritual and supernatural being. On this account his conscious life becomes absolutely worthless, or will become so if Positivism is permitted to triumph. Moreover, the annihilation of the influence of the Catholic church must remove all the restraints, established two thousand years ago upon the lusts of Paganism. These are about to arise from their graves, and stalk through the world in the foulest winding-sheets. Morality, art, personal dignity, therefore, all demand that a vigorous and determined resistance be at once offered to positive thought. This cannot be done by the force of reason, although it is quite untrue that Positivism has a monopoly of unbiassed reason. But it is impossible really to *prove* that religion is true. This fact, however, shows how ridiculous is the attitude of the Positivists in their fetish worship of truth and with their great doctrine of verification, since religion, which must be established without proof, is an infinitely more precious and valuable and beautiful thing than any of the numerous futilities which the Positivists have succeeded in proving. Religion reposes on three postulates placed one above another. You must admit that man is a moral being, and to do that you must not hesitate to contradict all the data and all the reasoning of Positivism. You must then admit that there is a God, and that man lives forever. And finally, since, after all, these admissions would do no good, except provisionally, and are of no practical use, you must go on and "admit" a special revelation to interpret and apply them, and admit further that Catholicism is the only revelation which can be said in any consistent manner to sustain the character of one.

Whatever the final opinion entertained of a book or of an author, the first impression of it depends a good deal upon the previous ideas existing in the mind of the reader. Sometimes these refer to the subject, sometimes to previous acquaintance with the character of the method. We confess that some prepossessions of this latter sort have lent a certain bias to the expectations with which we approached the perusal of this, the most serious volume that was as yet issued from Mr. Mallock's pen; for we had read the others; we knew the graceful pessimism of his "New Republic," the coarser, much coarser raillery of his "New Paul and Virginia;" the peculiar paradoxes of his *Nineteenth Century* essays. From these various studies we had derived a certain impression of Mr. Mallock's style of thought and drift of argument, impression that is now deepened and confirmed by the more ambitious effort which now invites our attention.

The nature of his subject, the titles of the different parts into which he divides it, the pathos of his apprehensions, the apparent fervor of his rhetoric, the piquancy of his eloquence, all suggest a thinker, serious, profound, yet sensitive; one who, below the superficial currents of popular opinion and popular applause, perceives the deep undertow that sweeps back to the sea, whose note of warning is shrill with sincere and well founded alarm. But on the other hand, these abounding metaphors, this incessant appeal to sentiment, the very variety of this rhetoric with its frequent flippancies, this drawing-room brilliancy of epigram, these smart sayings, this facile picturesqueness, suggest the doubt that the writer be really adequate to a theme so grave, so vast. Somewhat closer inspection detects many flaws in the enamel of the picture: inaccuracies of expression, more noticeable in a person who trusts so much to his gift of expression: negligencies of language, less pardonable where language is so facile and fluent; infelicities of metaphor, betraying false perception, and even obtuseness of imagination, serious defect in a scheme of philosophical presentation that consists almost entirely in an appeal to the imagination. When we exchange our surface inspection of the style for an analysis of the thought, we find that these superficial defects, continue uninterruptedy into deeper strata of character. We find that the striking but impossible metaphor often conceals an extraordinary slovenliness of thought; that the rhetoric is often so divorced from reality, that it fails to rise into eloquence; that an argument professedly basing itself on higher considerations than truth, can hardly fail to awaken supicions of insincerity, and, by the very professions of the writer, of voluntary manipulations of plain things, in the interest of a higher cause. We are reminded of those secret tribunals of the holy office, to which people were carried blindfolded, having been kidnapped on specious pretences. We cannot refrain from having something of the same feeling about Mr. Mallock as is always excited by the view of a policeman in plain clothes. We feel that he is on a mission, and that *he* is convinced his highest duty consists, not in acquiring a thorough understanding of the subject before him; but in securing at any price a victory for the powers whose instructions he obeys. Whatever the appearance of candid inquiry and impartial investigation, we feel that Mr. Mallock really looks at positive thought, very much as a British general looks at a Zulu; and his business in regard to it, is simply to compel a surrender. He tells us himself that "even the Pope is disposed to look upon Positivism as a belligerent rather than as a rebel." (p. 204.) In accordance with this attitude, military rather than philosophic, Mr. Mallock often betrays a bluff ignorance of the real nature of the doctrine he is discussing, quite analogous to that which the British soldier is not ashamed to manifest in regard to the topography of an enemy's country.

Thus, of the characteristics which go to the making of that type so bitterly well known in Europe—the Jesuit—Mr. Mallock, almost by his own showing, is at once seen to possess two; an habitual attitude of warfare, and a systematic and avowed contempt for truth. To these we may add a third more subtle, and not at first sight so obvious, peculiarity; we mean a predominant preoccupation about sexual sins. Mr. Mallock's other writings, to which we have alluded, already reveal this preoccupation. His criticism of Burne-Jones and Alma Tadema is unpleasantly suggestive of the famous Tartuffe scene, where Dorinda is requested to draw closer her kerchief. Mr. Mallock's imagination is not quite clean, and, as we have already suggested, it has received a permanent impress from meditation on the primitive relations between the church and a world plunged in sensual excess. Thus the waning influence of the church at once suggests to him a resurrection "of the buried lusts of Paganism," although at another time, by a singular inconsistency, he fears that Positivism will so weaken all vigorous impulses, that not enough will remain to afford employment for the repressing agencies of either reason or religion. The imaginary dialogue with Tyndall, which we have quoted in full, shows how instinctively Mr. Mallock reverts to this theme as to a central problem*—a problem that he cannot conceive of as soluble, except by means of the elaborate fictions invented, and often indeed usefully employed, by the Catholic church.

A fourth trait of Jesuitism, inherent in Mr. Mallock's principles—or else acquired early in the course of his conversion—is the conviction of the legitimacy of persecution as a means of bringing in lambs to the church, when all other means fail. This conviction is not formally announced in the present volume. But in a recent essay in the *Nineteenth Century*, in the series to which Mr. Mallock himself sends us for the complement of his thought,† we find the theory of persecution systematically defended. Whenever, he says, the immense majority of the wise and good in the community become unanimously agreed upon any doctrine, and convinced of its supreme importance, it is their duty to enforce this doctrine by all necessary means of compulsion.‡ Mr. Mallock rejects the torture, and other means of physical punishment, apparently because they are too vulgar, and have excited too much prejudice. He insists that the right of interference with private judgment is reserved by all governments, to a greater or less degree; and that the right claimed by the church

* Which we are far from denying it to be.
† See preface.
‡ See *Ninteenth Century*. 1878.

only extends so much further, as the importance of eternal salvation extends beyond the importance of the temporal welfare of a state. But as this is, on Mr. Mallock's hypothesis, an infinite extension, it is evident that the rights which may be claimed under it are dangerously, immeasurably large.

We would remark in passing, that as no speculative doctrine that was ever broached, can be accused of one thousandth part of the bad consequences which practical experience on the most vast and doleful scale has proved to flow from the doctrine of the right of persecution, as, moreover, this is an opinion in which, at the present day, an immense majority of the wise and good are quite agreed, it follows that, by a rigid application of Mr. Mallock's principle, the Home Secretary would be more than justified in at once arresting him as promulgator of a most pestilent heresy, and consigning him to the Tower for the rest of his active life.

In the volume before us, Mr. Mallock feels that one of the greatest difficulties in the way of commending Romanism to a nation to whom "Bloody Mary" and the Popish Plot are still realities, lies in the reputation for cruelty which Romanism has earned for itself. It is absolutely necessary to whiten this reputation, and this is the way Mr. Mallock does it: "There is no point probably," he says, "about which the general world is so misinformed and ignorant, as the sober but boundless charity of what it calls the anathematising church. * * * Never was there a religious body except the Roman, that laid the intense stress she does on all her dogmatic teachings, and had yet the justice that comes of symathy for those that [who] cannot receive them. * * * Her anathemas are on none but those who reject her with their eyes open, by tampering with a conviction that she is really the truth. These are condemned, not for not seeing that the teacher is true, but because having really seen this, they continue to close their eyes to it. They will not obey when they know they ought to obey, and thus the moral offence of a Catholic in denying some recondite doctrine, does not lie merely, and need not lie at all, in the immediate bad effects that such a denial would necessitate, but in the disobedience, the self-will and the rebellion that must in such a case be both a cause and a result of it." (p. 283–285.)

Yes, we know, and all Europe knows, the deadly claws which lie concealed beneath the soft velvet of this gentle distinction! We know that it means that the church denies itself the luxury of persecuting savages whom it is easy to baptise; but is compensated by full authority over all those born within the pale of its own dominions, *i. e.*, in all countries included under the title of Christendom. For the Peruvian heathen, the baptismal font; for the baptised European heretic, the spy, the tribunal, the thumb-screw, the rack, the dungeon, the oubliette, the stake.

> "And all we know, or dream, or fear
> Of agony, are thine!"

May the deep shudder of horror which has convulsed the inmost consciousness of Europe on this subject, never cease to vibrate so long as vitality remains in this deadly principle,—authoritative care of souls, to the salvation of man and the greater glory of God!

Yes, we know the type, whether male or female, the stealthy step, the set composure, the downcast eyes, the insinuating voice, the half perceptible deprecatory gesture with which dispute is declined when the proposition advanced has failed of a favorable reception, the apparent acquiescence, the secret resistance, watchfulness and counterplotting, by aid of a silent impersonal agency, invisible, ubiquitous, unfathomably treacherous: whose very good seems evil from the impossibility of testing its sincerity, whose evil seems blacker from its mantle of immaculate good;—who does not know this hated and hateful type, everywhere the same in essence under any disguise, under the priest's cassock or the nun's robe or the cardinal's hat? No Methodist fanaticism, no Baptist uncouthness, no Calvinistic rigidity, no Episcopal inconsistency, ever has or ever can awaken the passionate antagonism aroused by the vision of Jesuit Catholicism in the breasts of those who, either personally or in sympathy with her victims of any age, have known what it was to writhe, though but for an instant, in her clutches. She is still the Infamous, and, for our part, we should rue the day when modern toleration ever so far forgot its history as to remove the brand from this gigantic impersonal Personality.

Mr. Mallock wilfully belittles the matter when he asserts that Protestants reject Catholicism merely through ignorance of her true doctrines, as that of Biblical inspiration, of orthodoxy and the like. Nor does he confound Protestantism when he points out its inconsistencies, its speculative absurdities, its practical limitations and the vulgarity of many of its innumerable sects. Nor when he shows that the movement which "denied the authority of the church to assert the Bible," is the same as that which, carried somewhat further, "has denied the Bible to assert God, and has denied God to assert the dignity of man." We believe, indeed, contrary to the opinions of Comte, who despised Protestantism as thoroughly as Mr. Mallock does, that its disintegrating movement was indispensable even for the establishment of a new unity, destined perhaps to rival that of Catholicism. The essential worth of Protestantism is not in its speculative creed, confessedly identical in all essentials with that of Catholicism, but in its practical assertions of manliness, in its effective emancipation from slavery. We should hesitate to repeat what has been said so often and is so well known, were it not that writers from two opposing schools—those of Mr. Mallock's stamp—and others from among the Positivists, are constantly reviving the same superficial charge of inconsistency, constantly persuading others to forget the immense service rendered to humanity by the brave and determined revolt against the deadliest tyranny and foulest corruption, which movement calls itself Protestantism. Catholicism is a creed, a history and a life; Protestantism is no creed, but it is a life and a history; and it still stands pitted against its ancient opponent with all the just vehemence of vigorous life and with the burning recollections of real history. Its active vanguard calls itself now by other names—Free Thought, Rationalism, Positivism;* its humbler rear-guard is often composed of the middle class—Philistines and "Hebrews," at which Mr. Arnold sneers so profusely. It has many ridiculous prejudices, many untenable doctrines, but it has honest instincts, and still, we trust, virile fighting power. That these need still to be alert to resist an enslavement more effeminate, though for the moment more plausible and less cruel than the ancient one, is sufficiently proved by this latest insidious attempt to weave into an immense net this velvety tissue of worn-out sophistries, and throw it over modern Anglo-Saxondom, to ensnare if possible, the timid, the uncertain, the ignorant, the superstitious the hysterical.

We have purposely begun at the climax of Mr. Mallock's argument instead of at the beginning, and this for two reasons. In the first place, it is a kind of argument which can only be thoroughly appreciated when its real tendencies are completely known; and at the outset these tendencies are most carefully concealed. The author professes to be interested in nothing but "natural

* Of course we do not really overlook the technical differences between Rationalism and Positivism proper.

Theism," and on this ground is enabled to invite a number of people to meet him, who could never be persuaded within earshot of his real position. Then having (apparently) established "natural religion" by a "scientific argument," and by "exact thought," he makes a sudden change of base, and shows them that "these highest hopes, this precious creed," which was to save them from being "engulphed in mindless desolation," is after all worthless. It cannot *pass* without a "rider" in the form of a special revelation of Catholic theology. When this conclusion is once clearly appreciated at the outset, much of the energetic rhetoric that adorns the early pages falls flat. We know that it is not intended to mean what it says, except with certain mental reservations. We are not told at the outset what grand scheme of thought Mr. Mallock expects to oppose to that he undertakes to disintegrate; we are gradually manipulated, and led on from admission to admission, until finally we find ourselves exactly opposite our starting point.

Now this fact is of importance because we do not address these modest pages to Mr. Mallock himself, but to certain among his readers. One class of these are liable to a disagreeable shock of surprise when they discover that the final result of Mr. Mallock's "science," and the peroration of his eloquence is only a tender adjuration to return to the worship of the Virgin Mary. Unaccustomed to ritualistic litanies, the phrases, "Parent of sweet clemency," and "protecting from the enemy," fall on their ears with a strange and unwelcome sound. The personification of the church, the persistent attribution of feminine qualtities to "her," the description of "her" "putting away" of untenable doctrines, "not in petulant anger, but with a composed determined gentleness, as some new light gravely dawns upon her;" to a large class of readers all this will seem so effeminate as to be ridiculous, and the judgment of a person who prizes such effeminacies cannot but lose prestige with them; even when in the intricacies of the early polemic, they had been disposed to admire his subtlety, acuteness and depth. Such persons are habituated to consider Catholicism, and the appeal to an infallible church, as an issue entirely closed; and any one advocating them as one raised from the dead, not worth hearing when history and reason had already pronounced so decisively. The wish to obtain a true perspective for the vision of this class of readers, is therefore our first reason for reversing his order in examining Mr. Mallock's line of argument.

The second reason also refers to Mr. Mallock's readers, but to a very different class from the first. These are they who, having become dissatisfied with some form of Protestantism, most probably one of its advanced, optimistic, rationalizing forms, have become much impressed with the promises of rest, comfort and joy held out by the "most venerable communion of Christendom." For reasons that have been often described, these persons find an irresistible charm in the thought that a great many millions of people for many hundred years have believed a certain thing. What that thing may be is of secondary importance. Intrinsically the belief in witch-craft, almost coextensive with the belief in the Catholic theology, should be able to afford the same mysterious consolation. It is these persons who experience that same kind of pleasure in the personification of the church as is at present so largely afforded by the revival of mediæval fashions. Above all, the class of minds we are speaking of, are habituated to judge of everything by reference to themselves; to its effects on their own feelings and states of mind. Whatever seems to them touching, or comforting or attractive, at once convinces them of its reality. This class of persons, therefore, is entirely disposed to listen to a teacher like Mr. Mallock, whose habitual test or rejection of doctrine is: This is very tiresome: or, this is very dangerous. It is indeed the class to which he himself belongs. It is the class quite capable of floating into the bosom of the Catholic church, on nothing more substantial than clouds of fragrant incense, or the sweet voices of boy choristers, or the rich colors of painted windows, or anything indeed that appeals,—even superficially, to their æsthetic tastes.

Now it is evident that to such persons, the fact that Mr. Mallock's lines of argument all converge in this narrow circle, authority, infallibility, submission to spiritual guides securing "grace and mercy through set channels," "idolatrous" worship of the Virgin Mary, this fact we say has in it nothing alarming. They look at it as a proof of the broad basis really offered by reason, (though not required by authority,) to the doctrines of the church, since an argument that starts however far away from it, is compelled to terminate within its limits. They have already reached that station in intellectual life, where the argument is sought, not before, but after the creed; whatever seems to confirm this is eagerly accepted, whatever tends to cast a shadow on it is thrown aside. This class of people would be extremely uninteresting to us but for one reason. Besides the superficial and æsthetic needs, which they are ready to proclaim, there are others, logical, and far more profound, and of which they are often unconscious, but which command our respect. These are the needs of unity, of conscious membership in some mighty social body, of definite and dignified personal function, of occupation for exalted thought, of assured basis for conviction, of scope for tender and passionate sympathies. These are the needs that Catholicism offers to satisfy. These are the needs that Catholicism *has* satisfied in the past, and so long as these longing souls look exclusively to the past, they will find means of denying all the accusations which may be brought against it. They will say that Jesuitism is belied, and moreover that Catholicism is not all Jesuitism; that the errors, even to the rack, of which the mediæval church may be convicted, were common to the age in which she existed, torture being a practice in civil as well as ecclesiastical tribunals;

that errors are "put away with a composed gentleness," yet the spirit of the church remains the same; and to those to whom this sameness is the great charm, this answer is all sufficient. Why then should the church not be sufficient for the future?

The answer is contained by implication, in a single sentence of Mr. Mallock's essay. "Now as to the minor premise that there is no proof of religion, we may concede, *at least provisionally*, that it is completely true." (p. 215.) It is often the fashion, it is a principle with Mr. Mallock, that while proof is justly demanded in matters of science, it is superfluous in matters of faith, and that a religion is even degraded when it is made to repose on a demonstration. There is indeed a profound sense in which this is true—sense to which we shall return later. But here we may say, that the degradation comes not when the proof is furnished, but when it is demanded. The principle of authority must be carved out of a single block and self-sustained; the first line of demarcation which appears to separate it into different parts, is the crack of doom: the first attempt to support it on anything but itself, on reason, or natural religion, on argument, is the insertion of one end of a wedge between the pillar and the solid earth with which it had seemed to be continuous,—a wedge destined to become a lever by which it will one day be overthrown.

The field for the legitimate exercise of the principle of authority is so wide, that it is always easy to distinguish by concrete examples its vigor from its decrepitude, its reality from its pretence. The child does not question the authority of the parent, the ignorant that of the savant, the landsman that of the sailor, the sick man that of the doctor, the weak person that of anyone who has acquired a sufficient ascendancy over him. It is in these cases, and not as a rule in those that Mr. Mallock imagines, that the proposition believed "leaves no room for doubt, forces on the mind an invincible conviction," seems as indubitably true as the testimony of the senses. We entirely agree with Mr. Mallock's estimate of what he calls the major premise in the principal "Positivist" argument. (p. 216.) So far from it being impossible "to be certain of anything but what can be supported by proof," there can be no doubt but several large classes of persons are much more capable of being certain in obedience to some authoritative statement, than they are of understanding the nature of proof. The question really is: When is this mode of arriving at a conviction of certainty desirable? and when is it possible?—and we may say further, that it is never desirable when it has ceased to be possible, and never possible after the question of possibility has once been seriously raised.

Everyone knows that the authority of the Catholic church was only slowly consolidated. Mr. Mallock himself gives us a little historical sketch showing how this was done.

"Let us suppose nothing, to start with, in the world

but a natural moral sense, and a simple natural Theism. * * * Approached in this way, the religious world will appear to us as a body of natural theists, all agreeing that they must do God's will, but differing widely amongst themselves as to what His will and His nature are. Their moral and religious views will be vague and dream-like, more dream-like than those of the Protestant world at present. Their theories as to the future will be but shadowy hopes and fears. Their practice in the present will vary from ascetism to the widest license. And yet in spite of all this confusion and difference, there will be amongst them a vague tendency to unanimity. Each man will be dreaming his own spiritual dream, and the dreams of all will be different * * * Men will begin to compare their dreams together, and try to draw out of them the common element, so that the dream may come slowly to be the same for all,—that if it grows it may grow by some recognizable laws; that it may, in other words, lose its character of a dream, and assume that of a reality.* We suppose therefore that our natural theists form themselves into a kind of parliament: The Church of Rome is, ideally if not actually, the parliament of the believing world."†

---

* This is Mr. Mallock's conception of reality!

† The real danger to authority from analysis of *its* growth and origin, may perhaps explain the otherwise inexplicable horror entertained by all branches of the church for researches on the development of life and the origin of man. Reason can afford to contemplate insignificant beginnings; but authority must, under penalty of annihilation, be from the beginning, complete and sacred, final. Who does not know the thrill of horror caused by the famous 15th and 16th chapters of Gibbon?

Taken in a more abstract and at the same time more limited sense, this is a correct naturalistic description of the origin and growth of the church. But when the moment has come that such a human origin to authority can be described, the time has ceased when this authority can impose itself as divine. For that to be possible, the origin must be forgotten as completely, as indeed that of the church was forgotten during the middle ages. To secure the complete triumph of authority, no other way of arriving at knowledge must be open, except that of submission to its dictates. To-day, the assumption of such authority as that which the Catholic church must claim for itself, ("The church's primary doctrine is her own perpetual infallibility," p. 277,) is as if a parent should try to perpetuate his original attitude to his child, grown-up: or a savant, to his unlettered disciple, become as wise as he; or a sailor to the landsman who has been before the mast, or the physician to the sick man who has been made clinical professor; or the tyrant to the weak man whose moral sinews have grown strong in hardy self-assertion. When Mr. Mallock, to his description of the church of Rome as a natural growth from human dreams, adds, "She is all this, but she is something more; she is not only the parliament of spiritual man, but she is such a parliament guided by the spirit of God," (p. 281), we are compelled to answer: "Time was when this assertion would have seemed as simple as the remark, the sun is in the heavens. *We* have not changed, because when anything is said to us that seems as obvious, or in regard to some matter that we know we know nothing about, we shall except it as unhesitatingly as ever mediæval Catholic accepted the dicta of a papal bull. It is the times that are changed; it is the voice of the preacher, who no longer is able to restrict himself to simple affirmation and exposition, but who tries, like you, to prop this with elaborate argument and demonstration. If your word is enough, this argument is superfluous; but if you must fall back upon argument, then your unproved word goes for nothing. You have tried to prove to us that our senses cannot be relied upon to tell us whether the sun is above the horizon. We find the reasoning inconclusive. After that, you tell us, on the simple authority of some one you know, that some crab-apple tree is bearing divine fruit. But as we find you reason badly on the subject where you have invited us to reason, by what inducement shall we be persuaded to set our reason aside when you tell us there is no further occasion for it? May we not suspect that this suppression of reason is intended rather for your convenience than for our advantage, or for the necessity of the case?" Mr. Mallock would insinuate, "Nevertheless you *wish* to believe, and you may, if you *will* to do so," and then he has no other resource but the iteration of the old dogmatisms, the repetition of the old dogma. He mistakes or pretends to mistake the sense of need of believing irrevocably upon *something*, for a providentially implanted longing for belief in one or two particular things, that he tells us after all, *may* be found to be the truth.

It is precisely at this point that Positivism joins issue most definitely with Catholicism, and with the whole system of thought that Mr. Mallock is advocating. Positivism addresses itself to the same real need, but with real things. It says: "You long for an irreversible basis of belief. Seek it in the realities of existence. There are two sources of knowledge, the senses and human consciousness.* Unable yourselves, it may be, to unfold doctrines from these sources, yet in the fact of such origin you may have an infallible criterion of doctrines. Two kinds may be at once rejected; those which profess to originate in some source other and higher than these; and those which professing to be derived from them, are found on examination to have no connection with them. But the rejection of doctrine is a matter of secondary importance; the first and vital essential is to build up doctrine and to establish a positive ground for thought, for action, and for life."

It is here, and at the very outset, that Mr. Mallock so singularly misrepresents Positivism. "Its premises," he asserts, "are two great denials,—a denial of a personal God, and a denial of a personal immortality." But Comte says, "So long as mankind persist in *trying to solve the questions* which characterize its period of infancy, it is absurd to reject the naïve method employed by the imagina-

* Or as Locke said, "the senses and reflection."

tion, the only method really suited to their nature. These spontaneous beliefs could only be radically extinguished in the proportion as humanity, better enlightened in regard to its capacities and its needs, has changed irrevocably the general direction of its researches." (Syst. de Politique Positive, 7, 1, p. 47). And again: "The true positive method consists in substituting the study of the invariable *laws* of phenomena, for that of their *causes* immediate or final; in a word, substituting the determination of *how* for that of *why*."

It is of the greatest importance to make this cardinal fact perfectly clear, both because it is systematically mystified by our author, and because the persons to whom he addresses himself have not, as a rule, requisite knowledge on the subject.

The ultimate basis of Positive Thought is found not in the material universe, but in the laws of the human mind. So soon as any real inquiry was made into these laws, one thing became evident namely, that the only objects ever really present to the mind, were the attributes of things, and the succession of phenomena. The Substance in which attributes were supposed to inhere is simply a convenient formula to signify their coherence into some definite individual or unit; it responds to nothing thinkable or mentally presentable. For, whenever a person tries to think of the substance or internal essence of any thing, he really thinks either of one of its attributes or properties, or of their assemblage. If he try to abstract his mind from these, he can only do so by calling up some new attributes, paler and vaguer than before, but still attributes, and stamping the sum of these with the name he had refused to the first collection. This, even for the simplest mental act of presentation. If, however, he attempts to go further, if he wish to discuss the nature of a substance, or to compare it with another, or to judge of it or understand it, he at once finds that he is discussing, and comparing and judging its attributes, through which alone he knows or can imagine anything about it.

Again, when he analyses a little further the mental conception of an attribute, he finds that it consists of one of two things: either an image, conceivably appreciated by one of the five senses; or the cause of some event or series of events. Thus, if we ascribe vastness, to some substance or personality, we have, during all the time that our minds are dwelling on this attribute, a more or less vague image in the mind, derived from the largest sensible objects with which we are acquainted, as the illimitable ocean, the overarching sky. If on the other hand we ascribe goodness to this personality, we think, if we think at all, of circumstances in which some sentient beings will be treated in a way that will render them conciously happy, and yet which will not infringe some law of things which we have learned to know elsewhere. These more abstract conceptions are often rendered vivid by the presence of a distinct mental picture which offers a concrete illustration of the quality in question; as when in thinking of hate, we picture a man striking a violent blow; or of compassion, we see, in imagination, a woman lifting up a starving infant to her breast. *

Thus finally, the conception of an attribute is resolved into that of a succession of phenomena, and the whole thinkable universe, or everything with which our minds can in any way occupy themselves, becomes resolved into impressions and actions, into pictures and events. Movement, shown to be so inseparable from physical life, is equally so from thought.

At the close of this analysis, the term substance remains exactly where it was at the beginning, a term, convenient, perhaps indispensable, certainly therefore to be retained, but one that adds nothing to our knowledge, and can in no way really influence our thoughts. This is equivalent to saying that it is unknowable and unthinkable. †

It would be as absurd to *deny* it, as to take the trouble to contradict the naïve jargon of the child who says, "I did it to-morrow." There is no question but what in the innumerable dicussions that have been held about substances, the speakers have had some ideas in their minds, but these have not been what they thought they were, since to be so would involve a contradiction of terms.

All this is the elementary psychology of the text

* This point has been well dwelt upon by C. E. Pierce, in his Illustrations of the Logic of Science.—*Popular Science Monthly*, 1878.

† This is the first element in our doctrine of the unknowable, so lucidly worked out by Herbert Spencer.

books. For our present purpose however, what is important, is the corollary,—inevitable, but so generally overlooked and misunderstood. This corollary appears when the foregoing analysis is applied to the two principal substances which have been postulated by the human mind,—God and the human soul.

According to the simple anthropomorphic hypothesis, God or the gods were merely concealed personages, in every respects analogous to the human beings, whose attributes offered the model for theirs. Human will being the only cause for events which experience positively demonstrated, it was perfectly natural for the events which evidently escaped this cause, to postulate another entirely similar. The gods of Greek polytheism, and the Jehovah of Jewish monotheism were perfectly thinkable: according to the philosophical experience of the time, no philosophical objection could possibly be urged against belief in them.

Positivism therefore, accords much more respect, for this, the first, and theological state of humanity, than for the metaphysical which succeeded it, and which is filled with contradictions. Here, a person or persons are denied, but a divine personality is retained, the eternal Substance, affirmed to be beneath and behind all the changing phenomena of the world. The Christian conception constantly oscillates between pure anthropomorphism and pure metaphysics. In regard to the first, Positivism simply says: It is not proved, we have no data for proof, and must wait for data before we can form an intelligible opinion. In regard to the second it says: This substance is as truly unthinkable as any other. It is as impossible to deny such an eternal Substance underlying the phenomena of the world and supporting its attributes, as it is impossible to *deny* a substance underlying the phenomena of light, or supporting the attributes of a tree. But in the one case as in the others, and for precisely the same reasons, all knowledge of the substance must consist in knowledge of the attributes and phenomena. The substance beneath the phenomena of the world can only be known in these phenomena; hence, faithful study of them will attain all that is attainable; while speculations on the substance in itself, must be barren of result, and unthinkable jargon. If we assume a central will as the efficient cause of the events of human history, the manifestations of that will must be inseparable from the events of that history. Even "revealed history" (so called), is not, and cannot be, a history of anything but human actions to which the hypothesis of a superhuman agent is simply added. When this addition is made in certain localities, as when we are told that Abraham prepared to murder his son because a divine voice spoke to him, it has been the custom for centuries to agree with Abraham. When however Mr. Freeman asserts the same thing, we believe indeed that he thinks so, but our belief extends no further in this than in the case of any hallucination of hearing contained in our insane asylums. Thus, the will of the invisible

Supreme Being, becomes confounded with the history of the invisible *Etre suprême*. Since everything that has ever been asserted about God, consists in facts of humanity, positive thought simply rests upon the indisputable, instead of pretending to soar into the region of the unthinkable, without result. It claims moreover that all that ever was really known or contemplated under the metaphysical method, is still retained as an object of contemplation and of infinitely more fruitful research under the positive method. "This everywhere substitutes the question of *how*, for the question of *why*." Thus, on the supposition of a providential direction to the development of human history, the Positivist studies as minutely as possible the succession of events, their apparent causal dependencies, their modifications, their consequences. The metaphysician on the contrary, remains enclosed within the barren assertion, "This is, has been, and will be, the design of Providence." But *what* is, has been or will be, he cannot know, except in so far as he follows the Positivist method of observation. The Positivist has no quarrel with the assumption of the metaphysician, except that it is useless, and often tends to substitute an apparent explanation, for one which can really be made available. But it lets this hypothesis alone as not, in any sense, being a working hypothesis.

To the second important substance, the soul, the same considerations apply—so far, at least, as concerns souls external to the thinker's consciousness, *i. e.*, all but his own. He knows human beings by their attributes and by the phenomena of their actions : he coheres this manifold knowledge into a unit, an individuality : this nexus of cohesion he calls the soul of the man he is talking to. His own soul he apprehends by a different method—by the operation of consciousness. This coheres the succession of more or less distinct thoughts and feelings and volitions into a unit of definite individuality and permanent identity with itself. But it is these internal phenomena in the one case, as it is the external phenomena in the other, which constitute the real subject of knowledge, —the soul is but the unthinkable substance. The attempt to think of it apart from its attributes, results as before, in framing a conception of paler attributes. As the theological conception of the substance of the world is a Person, simply an enlarged human being, so the theological conception of the soul is simply a ghost—a thin and pale human body.

The following is a good illustration of the way in which positive science analyses the consciousness of self-identity, not, as Mr. Mallock and his school suppose, by exclusive reference to the physiological phenomena which may accompany this consideration, but complementing this by minute observations of the phenomena of consciousness itself :

"Psychical life *commences* in the organs of the senses; it is a constant current which passes from without inwards into perception, and from within outwards into organs of movement. * * * Between the sensation and the motor-impulse is gradually formed an accessory sphere, and this sphere developing, extending, enlarging little by little, finally becomes itself a powerful and complex centre, which, in its turn, diminishes in many respects both sensation and movement—and in the midst of which moves the entire spiritual life of man. This sphere is the sphere of the intelligence. * * * All effort, instinct, and volition represent the centrifugal motor force of the activity of the soul. The individual constitution of this aspect of the life of the soul forms in great part what we call personal character. * * * In the course of progressive life, thanks to the progressive liaison of ideas, there are gradually formed great compounds of ideas—more and more completely consolidated. * * * The child already receives from its relatively simple compounds of ideas a general impression, which he begins, as soon as he possesses the necessary elements, to designate under the abstract expression *I*. The *I* is an abstraction in which the traces of each of the previous sensations, thoughts and volitions are contained, enfolded, and which, in the ulterior course of psychic processes, is constantly renewed. This assimilation of new perception to the preëxistent *I* is not made suddenly, but in slow progression. * * * Our *I* is at different epochs very different from itself. According to the age, to the various duties of life, to events, to momentary excitements, such and such compounds of ideas which at any given moment represent the *I* develop themselves more than others, and place themselves in the first rank." *

To the question, "Why can the soul be connected with the body?" Positivism answers: 1st. No question of *why* in regard to the ultimate facts of existence can ever be answered; we can only show *how* two facts may be mutually dependent or describe their interaction. 2d. The term "soul" is not an abstract term corresponding to an individual group of attributes which may be contrasted with those corresponding to the "body." On the contrary, universal experience shows that it refers to a much more complex unity, into which the attributes of body always enter as constituent parts. There is therefore as little reason for inquiring *why* these two should be connected as why the color of a block of marble should be connected with its density.†

If again, the question is asked, "Will the soul survive the body?" Positivism replies that this is a question of a future series of events, for whose solution all our experience of past series affords no data. Science claims to be able to predict the future, only in so far as there is reason to suppose that its sequences will be uniform with those of the past. It does not deny the possibility of some brusque interruption of these sequences, com-

---

* Griesinger, Malad. Mentales. Trad. fran. pp. 28–54.

† The analogy of course is only partial, since the connections between the attributes appreciated by different senses differ essentially from that between an attribute perceptible by the senses and another appreciable by [mental] perception.

ing from some hitherto unknown source;* but with these, by the hypothesis, it can have nothing to do. Nor can knowledge of such events be obtained by an act of faith, as distinguished from an achievement of science. For faith only differs by acquiring knowledge on the strength of testimony, while science acquires it on the strength of demonstration. Anything, therefore, which could never be a matter of knowledge, could never be a matter of faith, since there would then be no one to give the requisite testimony. And in accordance with this, Theology, so long as it was unsophisticated by metaphysics, has always relied for proof of a life after death, on the testimony of those who had risen from the dead, and the central doctrine of Christendom was not an unthinkable isolation of the soul from the body, but the resurrection of the body with its usual complement of a soul.

Thus, to metaphysical conceptions of God and of the soul, Positivism opposes the remark, (made as Mr. Mallock would say, "not in petulant anger,") that these conceptions are unthinkable and therefore do not require to be discussed. If this remark seems "destructive," it is no more so than are the analyses of these same conceptions made, over and over again, by theologians and by metaphysicians themselves, as Mr. Mansel's famous Bampton Lecture on the "Limits of Religious Thought," would alone amply testify.

---

* Mr. Stanley Jevons, in his Principles of Science, has clearly shown the true scope of "scientific forecast."

To the simpler, theological conceptions, properly so called, Positivism opposes an entirely different remark. The conception of an invisible and gigantic man called God, and of an individual whose body is composed of an entirely thin material, exhaling from the old body like the breath, or disengaging from it like an insect from a chrysalis, and going to live in some invisible locality, all this is perfectly thinkable, perfectly intelligible, and not at all mysterious. It is a simple question of fact; and like every other question of fact must be settled by an appeal to one of two sources of information, the testimony of consciousness, or the testimony of the senses. But it cannot be settled by the testimony of consciousness, because it refers to facts external to the range of consciousness. It must therefore appeal to the testimony of the senses; that is to say, some one must have seen God, and some one must have seen the ghosts of persons who had died. We need scarcely remind our readers that it is precisely in this way that these "facts" have been established, from the Mosaic vision of Jehovah to the resurrection of Jesus Christ. Credence on testimony in regard to them, constantly more remote, has been the principle occupation of faith. While Protestantism embodies more metaphysical conceptions, so Catholicism being much more purely theological, is also more frankly anthropomorphic. By the inclusion of the Virgin Mary, "Parent of sweet clemency," its Godhead is quadruple instead of a Trinity; and the hierarchy of Saints is well known to fulfil all the functions of the demigods they displaced. The articles of faith in Catholicism contain, therefore, more of this simple description, questions of fact, reposing on historical testimony, and hence inevitably liable to just such demand for proof as meets other questions of fact.

In the absence of external proof therefore: in the absence of those movements of consciousness, which, as we shall see, replace external proof in matters *not* susceptible of it, Positivism simply lets these alleged facts alone, as it lets alone alleged metaphysical mysteries. There is no other sense in which any meaning could be found for the assertion, "Positive thought sets out from two great *denials.*"

On the contrary, Positivism has discovered, or rather it is itself the expression of the discovery, that the attainment of certainty means the establishment of a special relation between any human mind and the universe external to it, which relation may be established in two different ways. First, a scheme of things may be constructed, complete in itself, internally consistent, but which is never allowed to come in contact or contrast with the things themselves. It is perfectly well-known, that internal consistency and harmony, was the only test of truth known to antique thought; and that it supplemented the appeal to actual authority characteristic of mediæval thought. Such a faith is only foresworn, where accidental contact with the real things, has rendered too obvious for mistake, inadequacies or contradictions in the scheme. The way is then laid open for the second method. This consists in constructing a scheme of things, not at once, but gradually, and, at every step comparing it with the real things by performing some action on the real things which must fail, if the theoretical scheme be not in real accordance with them.

This was done on the vastest scale, when the Copernican was finally substantiated for the Ptolemaic system of astronomy. The series of verifications by which this magnificent achievement was affected, constitute, as is known a series of actions, sometimes purely mental, as calculations, sometimes involving visible circumstances, as navigations which must have failed had the Ptolemaic system been true, but by succeeding, proved it irrevocably to be false.

No Positivist thinker would ever wish to diminish the just emphasis laid by Comte, on the tested discovery of true astronomical laws, as the basis of all modern sense of truth. Comte considered the knowledge of these laws, and of the method by which they have been established, as the " indispensable preparation " to the Positivist conceptions of life ; and insisted that every child should be educated sufficiently to understand the demonstration. The Catholic however, still fails to perceive the true significance of these momentous discoveries ; or, like Mr. Mallock, sees in them no consequence more important than that the earth now-a-days, from its known relations to the solar system, appears somewhat smaller than it did before. Mr. Mallock sneers unmitigatedly at "this doctrine of verification," which is "the great fulcrum of the modern intellectual lever," and insists that it has no bearing upon matters alone worth caring about, namely, belief and religion. It is easy to show on the contrary, that the belief, now generally diffused, that the earth is round, and that the earth moves, offers such a perfect type of belief, that, since its acquisition, all beliefs claiming to be such, must be brought into comparison with it, in testing the reality of their claim. Thus this is, for the immense majority of those acknowledging it, and more or less consciously adjusting their lives to it, a belief upon testimony, and not a matter of knowledge personally acquired. Even the demonstration would be incomprehensible to these same persons, yet not the slightest doubt is felt of its correctness, because the testimony of all persons competent in the matter is absolutely unanimous in one direction. Hence the belief imposes itself with an authority scarcely attained, and certainly never surpassed by any dogma of the church in the days of its most complete ascendency. The objects to which this belief relates, though conceivably sensible, are practically, immeasurably beyond the apprehension of the senses: the belief, though not technically abstract, as a belief in goodness or beauty or other abstract quality, is, relatively to the capacity of human imagination, quite as vast as such a supra-mundane concrete belief as that in a personal

God; and certainly much vaster than that in an individual life after death, or in the intercession of the Virgin Mary, or various other beliefs in the Catholic theology. This belief therefore possesses whatever characters of spirituality can possibly be assigned to such theological beliefs. To all those persons, therefore, who are longing for certainty, for the repose afforded by an irrevocable basis for belief, Positivism may say: "Here is a certain truth. The earth is round, and the earth moves."

We are well aware, if by chance we have succeeded in persuading any of Mr. Mallock's readers to follow us to this point, that this proposition is liable to be greeted with a burst of derision. "The earth is round! Well, what of it? The earth moves! We knew that in the primary school! What comfort, what moral guidance can possibly be derived from such a statement?"

Softly.—We did not say that this doctrine would meet *all* the needs we have enumerated as worthy of respect, and capable of being supplied by Positivism. We have, so far, only spoken of one, but that to which Mr. Mallock and all writers seeking to make proselytes to Catholicism most frequently appeal,—the need, namely, of *some* absolute truth announced by imposing authority. For those who find a comfort in authority, the cosmic theory of the earth they live in may surely afford as much exercise for faith and acts of submission as [for instance] the recently announced doctrine of the Immaculate Conception of the Virgin Mary, latest "petal on the half-blown rose" of Catholic doctrine. Or, if we listen to Mr. Mallock,—why should pure Cosmism be less attractive and influential than "purely natural Theism, with no organs of human speech, no machinery for making its spirit articulate." The poet may say,

> "God's in his heaven,
> All's right with the world,"

But the Catholic thinks this an unwarranted inference, until confirmed by much authoritative addition to the original statement. Theism, therefore, to the Catholic, must stand precisely on the same plane as do the fundamental facts of the cosmic theory. If the latter offer no moral guidance, neither, in itself, does the former.

The cosmic theory is not Positivism, but it is the basis of positive thought, as the illustration, on the vastest scale, of the complete success which may attend the study of phenomena quite irrespective of any substance or personality which might underly them.

The demonstration of the position and relations of the earth in space would seem at first sight to so immensely transcend the powers of the human intellect, and at the same time be so useful to human welfare, that, on theological grounds, we might justly expect it to be the theme of a special revelation. Yet no revelation was vouchsafed, and the achievement was accomplished by the human intellect alone, once working in accordance with the real laws of its constitution.

In the original demonstration, therefore, a second is implicitly contained, namely, that the human mind is correlative with the universe,*—is capable of really unravelling its intricacies, comprehending its relations, and predicting its events. And third consequence, not perhaps so closely connected with the first, the visible universe is shown to constitute a suitable medium for the activity of the faculties of the human mind—a real home for the human soul. Thus the influence of physical science is shown at the very outset to far transcend the scope of physical things. It is a compound into which enters much less the material objects whose relations it defines than the mind which discovers those relations. It furnishes the "indispensable basis of reality" required for the activity of human lives which *begin* in the senses, and extend so indefinitely far beyond them. But how, it will be asked with insistance, can these cosmic facts contribute to "moral guidance" or to "personal happiness?"

The knowledge of these facts destroys the cosmogony upon which the original anthropomorphic theology rested, and by so doing at once indicates the necessity of some new conception of things, without which no permanent tranquility is possible for human beings. The method of demonstrating these facts in the material world establishes by its success an important precedent for researches in the internal, spiritual or moral world.

* Whether or no this correlation be complete evidently remains to be seen. Possibly not.

It is established that the first way to arrive at truth is to ascertain what are the true relations of things. This method in the moral world consists in studying the actions to which moral approbation or disapprobation have become attached, in their relations to one another, to their personal or social antecedents and consequences, to the physical condition which may coincide with them: finally, to the ideals which have been created during the gradual evolution of the moral world. The moral law becomes understood as the science of such relations. It as little resembles a "code of restraining orders," proclaimed from the top of Mt. Sinai, or from the recesses of the Sybilline cave, as does the law of gravitation. It cannot therefore be "revealed" or "announced;" it must be slowly and laboriously built up; it must expect to change somewhat with the slow changes which are constantly shifting the social relations that form such a large part of its basis. It has an internal coercive force derived from the consciousness of the sentient beings who are subject to it, and who, when in a normal condition, cannot but desire to act in accordance with the laws of their normal existence; and it has an external coercive force derived from public opinion, which, in the interest of the larger existence of society, constantly tends to compel to the normal condition the deviations from it of which abnormal individuals may be guilty. When the sense of social law is lost, no force remains capable of exercising this compulsion; social existence is threatened to the extent of the permitted deviation, and, as repeated experience has shown, may be completely dissolved on account of it.*

Thus far the moral law may be studied and established by the methods employed with indubitable success in the physical sciences, and first learned from them. But as it belongs to a different world, it is to be expected that it should possess in addition a method especially characteristic. And it has. Consciousness does not merely register, it creates—creates out of a mass of most complex material, furnished from many sources, but creates, nevertheless, something different from them. The moral standard prevailing at any given epoch of society, and to which individual actions are more or less completely compelled to conform, is an ideal which, if long maintained, must be in accordance with the general conditions of existence of that society, and especially with its speculative beliefs. But it is in itself its own excuse for being; it is the product of the free creative (though unconscious) impulse of the human beings making up that society; it is the ultimate goal towards which such impulse is directed. An ideal once created, as of honor, or purity, or order, tends to impose itself by an internal coercive force, derived from the correspondence of the ideal to a certain degree

* By this it is not meant that the extensive violation of the moral law is the only cause of social dissolution, but only an efficient one. A community may be broken up by a pestilence which destroys its commercial relations, and thus cuts off its supply of food, or by the dissolute and immoral habits generated during the prevalence of a pestilence, which however, conceivably, could be resisted by an heroic moral sense.

of development of society. The higher the ideal, the higher the development, and conversely, so that ultimately the moral force coalesces with and is sustained by the force of existence, constantly tending to enlarge. Thus this second part of the moral law is strictly analogous to the æsthetic law.

A given social development will involve a given ideal of art, whose beauty, inappreciable to members of a lower society imposes itself without question in its own sphere. Thus, the Dresden Madonna, which says nothing to a Bushman, needs no proof of greatness to enrapture a European. And thus again, the constant love for one woman which belongs to the high type of modern marriages, is a folly in the eyes of the licentious, whose existence in modern society is a survival of lower forms, and can only be tolerated because it occupies, after all, a minor part in it.

It is in this branch of morals and in art that we may justly say, *Proof* is not necessary to establish truth. But we shall presently see by what a juggle Mr. Mallock takes this principle from the field in which it is applicable to another, where it makes absolute nonsense.

To compass the wide range of the Moral Law, in its two parts of Demonstration and Creation, is no more given to every one than is the correlative task of compassing the demonstrations of science, or of rising to the creations of art. This is done by leading intellects, and the results at which they arrive, summed up in principles and in precepts, which, having received the sanction of public opinion, gradually become part of the social consciousness, and of that of each member of society. It is the èlite of artists, scientists and philosophers which really constitute that "Parliament of spiritually minded men," which Mr. Mallock labors to restrict to so much narrower significance. The Parliament of the church limits its discussions to a technical circle of questions, real interest in which the world has entirely outgrown. The universal Parliament extends its inquiries in every direction that human thought may reach. The first begins with assuming on the basis of tradition, that certain concerns are vital, and then is obliged to devote a large part of its energies to compelling the world to feel their vitality. The second takes up those interests whose vitality manifests itself indubitably in the very tumult and disturbance they occasion, and strains to trace out their relations to the fundamental conditions of existence. The church Parliament avowedly disdains the very world in which it sits and operates, and its uniform answer to inquiry concerning the right direction of terrestrial forces, or the legitimate adjustment of mundane preoccupations, is to let both alone. The Parliament of Humanity, conscious of a responsible mission in behalf of a powerless constituency, devotes laborious days to seeking out, among the intricacies of a marvellous universe the multiple response to the innumerable needs of man.

Still remains the question: This mission may perhaps

satisfy the élite members of this Parliament; but what is to be the real occupation of that immense "constituency." The church, while elaborating its dogma, to be offered to the faith of the masses, has known how to occupy these and assign to each a place. Under the regime of Positivism, what are the masses to do, while science is achieving its demonstrations, and art is elaborating its ideals?

The answer to this question can only be found by comparing with the vast communion offered by the church, the still vaster organism contemplated by Positivism.

At the beginning of Mr. Mallock's chapter entitled "Sociology as the formation of morality," he quotes from Prof. Clifford the remark: "Society is the highest of all organisms; and its organic nature is one of those great facts which our own generation has been the first to state rationally."

This is indeed a great fact, and it is a cardinal fact in the "Cours de Philosophie Positive" from which Mr. Mallock might more appropriately have quoted it. In referring to it Mr. Mallock seems to assume, that the exact nature of an organism is perfectly well understood, first by his readers, and second by himself. To judge by the consequences he deduces from the doctrine of "organic" social relations, we should infer that this second proposition was at least doubtful. It is possible therefore that the first is equally uncertain, in which case some preliminary definitions will not be superfluous. An organism is a complex unit, susceptible of progressive evolution, whose several parts are successively subordinated to one another, and each of which sustain a double current of activities; those necessary for the integrity of the individual existence; and those which contribute to the maintenance of the larger individual, in which the smaller is included. An organism is not a mere agglomeration of individuals, nor can it be adequately pictured by any one of them, nor does their maintenance constitute its function, for it can have no function except in so far as it may itself enter into the composition of a larger organism. On the contrary the organic elements have no significance if deprived of their relations to one another, and of their functions in the organism they compose. If therefore society be an organism, as Mr. Mallock appears to admit, it is quite incorrect to say, "that it neither does nor can mean anything but a number of happy individuals, so organized, that their individual happiness is secured to them." (p. 51.) No one familiar with the science of Biology from which the conception of an organism has been derived, would dream of saying: "The social organism is like a yew tree. Science will explain how it has grown up from the ground, and how all its twigs must have fitting room to expand in, but will not show us how to clip the yew tree into a peacock." (p. 59) This is the true Catholic conception of living things, as something to be clipped and tortured into a form that is the most remote possible from the natural one. The biological conception suggests no interference but such as shall secure the most complete and harmonious development of the yew tree, in its own form.

Of so complex an organism as society, an animal body is the only adequate type. In it, individual human beings may be compared to individual cells; the primitive natural groups of families to tissues; the larger groups of classes ranks, orders, etc., correspond to organs, by means of which the life of society is immediately carried on. To know therefore what is essential for human beings, we must first consider what is essential to their prototypes, organic cells. For these three things are essential, nutrition, reproduction, function.

Nutrition is required, first to maintain the statical integrity of the cell; second to provide for its growth and reproduction; third to render possible its function. The nutrition of a human being must be divided into two kinds: the nutrition of the body and that of the soul, or in other words, satisfaction of physical, and satisfaction of mental or spiritual wants. Many spiritualistic persons, Mr. Mallock we presume among the number, will be ready to eliminate from the present discussion all consideration of physical nutrition, because, in the analysis of happiness, such vulgar satisfactions are presupposed. But that the question of this physical nutrition cannot properly be so eliminated will appear when we consider: First that the sentiment of well being, the equilibrium and effectiveness of the moral as of the physical nature, is so largely dependent upon physical nutrition, including under this term not only food, but the physical health which should be secured by food. Second, that the task of wresting from a not too bounteous nature the means of physical nutrition, constitutes the primitive occupation of man, cannot be abandoned so long as he inhabits this planet, and so far from becoming easier, constantly tends to increase in difficulty, and the intricacy of the means employed, must therefore, to a constantly large extent, absorb the energies of the human race. The habitual oblivion of this fundamental fact, is a curious characteristic of the drawing-room school of philosophers to which Mr. Mallock belongs. These all reason about human nature with the same airy unconsciousness of the practical conditions of its existence, as do the luxurious talkers in the "New Republic," who sport with philosophy during the interval between the lunch served by the gilded footman, and the dinner provided by the competent butler. "Why should the people starve when there are such delicious *brioches* to be had for a sou a piece?" "How can the human race be satisfied with undisturbed ennui and soulless sensuality; when the social machinery has come to run more smoothly, and the rose-leaves been better laid." (p. 72.) We reply that the real satisfaction of the physical needs of *all* the human race, as they never have been hitherto satisfied, would and does leave little time for "undisturbed ennui" except among those who continue to avoid the necessity of getting their own living by making some one else work for them.

Such disturbance of equilibrium as this evasion occasions is not possible in a material organism, but only too possible to the social, and source of many of its gravest disorders and widespread individual unhappiness. The homely and oft-quoted advice to the rich hypochondriac, "Live on sixpence a day and earn it," contains a truth so profound as to be worthy of place in at least a practical philosophy. It is the full recognition in however bizarre a fashion, of this necessarily industrial basis for life, that gives such immense value to the socialistic system of Fourier.*

The provision for physical nutrition is thus inseparable from that for moral sustenance, and that by a circumstance not peculiar to man, but to which he submits in common with all animals. For moral nutrition comprises three needs,—the need for occupation, for knowledge, for sympathy. Now the first occupation offered to the faculties of any animal—man included—is that of procuring food. This elementary want satisfied, others arise, of all degrees of refinement and complexity, but which, so long as they are simply expressions of instinctive tastes or passions, or of desire of appropriation, remain within the class typified by the desire for food. After that,—the need of occupation is met during the process of satisfying other needs,—either secondary, as the nutri-

* Essentially different from the "communistic" systems, where the emphasis is laid, not on working for the goods, but on sharing them.

tive needs of knowledge and sympathy, or primary, as the needs of reproduction and function.*

The second need of moral nutrition is the desire for knowledge.

The most rudimentary sentiment about knowledge is the desire to utilize it in the attainment of an end, and, of course, first the primitive ends of self-maintenance and self-defence. But long before this utility has been exhausted, the sentiment of interest in knowledge for its own sake has been aroused. It certainly possesses considerable vivacity at this stage of development at which we are now contemplating human beings, when they have become conscious members of a social organism. The desire for knowledge, and the capacity for acquiring knowledge, varies as extensively as the capacity for work. It ranges from the merest rudiment, as existing in the curious savage, to the powerful and absorbing passion of the civilized scientist. That Mr. Mallock should entirely omit this desire, and the intense delights attendant upon its satisfaction from the enumeration of the "goods" left available for a race that should have ceased to anticipate the joys of heaven, seems to us very singular.†

* "C'est un fait vrai. bien que triste à dire pour des gens civilisés que la faim et l'amour sont les motifs les plus puissants qui dirigent toutes nos actions." Griesinger, loc. cit., p 44.

† Yet two far greater writers than Mr. Mallock have been guilty of the same omission. Fourrier was so much absorbed in the task of assigning adequate scope for energies, industries, and passions, that he has failed to notice that the desire of knowledge may become a passion. He allows two and a half hours a day as the utmost limit of time which the most studious person would desire to pass in the library. Comte, on the other hand, was

It is another illustration of the unnecessary penury of resource to which is reduced a thinker, who substitutes pursuit of an abstract "Higher Good" for the real, concrete, manifold goods for which human nature is so eager.

It is in the life of the laboratory, where the secrets of nature are not only divined but reproduced, that the true joy of knowledge can best be learned. Certain it is that from the laboratory this joy has been diffused with immeasurably greater rapidity and intensity than ever was the case where the library was the only centre of diffusion.

The true Positivist conception goes beyond that of Comte. While recognizing with him the inferiority in force of the intellectual faculties as compared with that of the emotions and passions, it recognizes that these are necessary to complete the self-consciousness of the individual—at least in all classes above the lowest. It pro-

---

too thoroughly pre-occupied, with his own passion for discipline and for unity,—passion inherited from Catholicism,—to either sincerely sympathize with or to sincerely believe in genuine intellectual activity among the masses. Indeed he dreaded it, as tending to "anarchy" of opinion and morals;—asserted that it was only possible under the stimulus of some passion, which by the force of public opinion should be restricted to the passion for the welfare of humanity. If this passion were not dominant, egotistic passions would certainly be the real motive for this pretended search after truth for its own sake. All this sounds unpleasantly like the "rebellion, disobedience, and self-will" of the Catholic discipline. But Positivism, however justly grateful to Comte, has outgrown his limitations. Its modern disciples, naturalists rather than mathematicians, have tasted such delights in acquisition of knowledge of the material universe, as Comte never knew. His own profound joy of knowledge, he could not imagine as shared by the masses of men whom he looked upon as so immeasurably beneath him. But Huxley and Tyndall are never tired of trying to impart such delight, as far as possible to the unlearned and common people.

poses a systematic substitution of science for faith, and the habit of demonstration for the habit of credulity, as far as this may be possible, in each individual case. The fundamental effort of education should be directed towards making every mind reflect some portions of the realities in which it is immersed. The extent of knowledge so reflected may vary infinitely, from the modicum just above what is necessary to direct the tiniest personal life, to the vastest range of speculation; but the nature of the pleasure, so different in degree, is the same in kind. It is only those who have really for themselves mastered some portion of knowledge, that are able to contrast their modicum with the immense range that escapes mastery. It is precisely this contrast which incessantly reproduces for each person making it, that impression of the infinite from which Mr. Mallock and his school are so fearful lest we escape.*

As is the case with the need of occupation, so the need for knowledge may not only be gratified in and for itself, but in connection with other needs. The desire for knowledge originates occupation for its fulfilment; the possession of knowledge offers a field for the occupation of thoughts, and also renders possible further occupations and the fulfilment of function. Finally, knowledge deepens sympathies, and, in widening, widens the range of existence in every sphere.

* This simple observation, taken in the abstract, contributes to that doctrine of the unknowable to which we have already had occasion to refer.

The third need which we have defined as belonging to moral nutrition is the need of sympathy. By this we mean the need of coming into emotional relations with fellow beings. Sympathy in this wide sense signifies the entire range of feelings whose gratification necessitates the presence and coöperation of one's fellows. Thus self-complacency, vanity, pride, ambition, all legitimate within a certain limit, are passions inconceivable except in social beings; society is as necessary for their satisfaction as for that of love, friendship, tenderness, benevolence, often alone suggested by the term of sympathy. By the above definition we may even include antipathies, and see in them, as did Fourier, the analogues of the musical discords required for the development of complex harmony.

To modify a little a remark of Mr. Mallock's already quoted—sympathy reduced to a single species would be like a pianist whose key-board was reduced to a single octave. It really embraces the entire range of feelings developed from the primitive need of escape from primitive solitude—the need for one human soul to live in the life and thoughts of another—need so universal, so profound, that to thousands its satisfaction suffices for happiness, notwithstanding all other moral privations.

The foregoing considerations already show that human beings are at least as narrowly dependent on their organic relations as are the elements of any material organism. In these the nutritive phenomena of assimilation cannot be studied, without taking into account the nutritive currents, coming from without and dominated, not only by local circumstances, but by the circulation and innervation common to the entire organism. So the various hungers, occupations, knowledges, sympathies of the human cell, which we have likened to movements of individual cellular nutrition, because they sustain its personal moral existence, cannot be thought of without the correlative of other persons, and of a larger social life whose central events dominate the local events around each individual.

Of the second primary need, that of reproduction, we need say little more than is necessary to signalize the fact that it *is* a primary necessity with all living beings, and preëminently so with human beings, in whom the instinctive love of offspring is reënforced by so much that is most powerful, in feeling, in thought, and in habits of action. Those who stand outside the regular line of succession of the human race are the least fitted to pronounce upon its needs, its capacities for virtue or happiness, the prizes towards which its energies may direct themselves. The celibacy of the Catholic clergy, though Mr. Mallock assures us that its expediency is only "a pious opinion," confers a stamp of immense significance upon its body of doctrine, and would alone suffice to consign that to a completely artificial sphere. But this is a well worn theme. Instead of dwelling upon it, we find it more profitable to notice that in this, as in so many other cases, human nature possesses double resources, and, when the first and simpler fails, can often supply the need with something more remote and more complex. Human beings do not reproduce themselves alone in their children, but in any creation of individual existence into which they have poured the force of their natures.

It is a fact, often commented upon, that the greatest geniuses, the greatest benefactors to humanity have so generally been celibate or childless, and often support the privation with little suffering. Even on a humbler scale than that of genius, it is possible, as thousands of modest lives daily testify, through the exercise of generous energies or the expansion of warm affections, to so sustain a real or an ideal life that it shall become like the reproduction of their own. In this task they may at once satisfy this primary longing of their individual nature, and enter into definite relation with the social organism, for whose maintenance, the incessant reproduction of elements is an essential.

It is, however, especially by means of its *function*, that individual elements, whether material or human, are most conspicuously connected with the organism to which they belong. The term function indeed has no meaning for the individual except in relation to the organism: it is thus distinct from the simpler term, activity, which we have already comprised under the need of occupation.

Further, individual function bears no resemblance to social activities. The function of a liver cell, secreting bile and sugar, does not offer any points of comparison with the activity of the man for whose benefit the secretion is accomplished

The elements of an organism have a function; the organism can have none unless it be itself considered as an elementary part in another organism. This is a fact of fundamental importance in the theory of the Social Organism, for it at once nullifies questions about the general aims and duties of society, which, in ignorance of the theory, are so often asked. Society exists; it manifests spontaneous activities, and possesses an inherent tendency to constantly develop its existence from a simpler to a more complex state; activity and tendency common to all organisms. Duty, morality, destiny, final purpose, are terms derived from the relations of its elements to it and to one another, relations so fundamental that they involve the conditions of social existence by defining the mode of coexistence of these organic elements. We cannot apply them to society as a whole, because we are acquainted with no analogous organism with which it may be brought into relation.

Mr. Mallock's failure to understand this theory entirely vitiates all he has to say on the subject of sociology, and even renders his definitions grotesque. "The social happiness of all of us, means nothing but the personal happiness of each of us." (p. 58.)

This, on the theory of the organism, (which, be it observed, Mr. Mallock thinks he admits), is as absurd a statement as would be one that the whole life of a man was patterned in that of one of the cells of his liver, and could be at once described by conceiving of an infinitely numerous agglommeration of these cells. But an organism is essentially characterized by the differentiation of its parts. A body whose cells all resemble each other in structure and in function, is not an organism but a honey comb.* What the parts have in common is the *fact* that they all possess a nutrition, are capable of reproduction, and perform a function ; but these differ as widely in each case as the nutrition and function of connective tissue cells differ from those of ganglionic bodies. So in society. The function of the coal heaver brings him as truly into relation with the social organism, as does that of the Secretary of State, since the business of heaving coals is quite indispensable to the welfare of society. But neither in matter nor in form, neither in difficulty nor in complexity, does it resemble, nor can it suggest the work of the higher official. In accordance with this we find that the nutrition of the coal heaver, when he is really suited to his work, and neither above or below it, is of a correspondingly different order. The physical nutriment he re-

* Upon this indisputable fact, some theories have, however, been constructed which afford much cause for dispute. The whole system of fixed social hierarchies and castes may plausibly invoke the organic conception of society in its favor. And, as is well known, it is in pursuing the doctrine of differentiation of function that Mr. Spencer has been led to support the theory of permanent and universal differentiation in the social functions of the sexes. We believe, however, that classifications of this kind are really as imperfect as is the caste system of India ; and much inferior to the more flexible system, which, in Europe and still more in America, tends to class individuals according to their real capacities they may manifest, instead of confining them irrevocably to the capacities of the class in which they were born.

gards is coarser; his occupation can, without detriment, be harsher and more monotonous, his knowledge much more rudimentary; his sympathies simple and grosser; consequently the "good" required by such a man can only be compared with the good required by the other, in the same way that a lower type can be compared with a higher of which it offers the rudimentary outline. It *is* true that

> "We are one flesh and need one flannel,
> With a proper difference as to quality."

The difficulty in appreciating the effect upon the individual happiness, of the consciousness of social function, is felt precisely in regard to the great mass of human beings, who, to any other view but the Positivist's, are not supposed to have any function at all.

It is conceded that a few quite exceptional persons may have this especial enjoyment, but it is by nature more limited than any other which is known. "Take the world as it is at present," says Mr. Mallock, "and the sense, on the individual's part that he is personally promoting its progress, can belong to and can stimulate exceptional men only, who are doing some public work. * * * The fact indeed that things in general do tend to get better in certain ways, must produce in most men, not effort, but acquiescence. It may, when the imagination brings it home to them, shed a pleasing light occasionally over the surface of their private lives; but it would be as irrational to count on this as a stimulus to further action, as to expect that the summer sunshine would work a steam engine." (p. 168.)

Again an illustration of the way in which our author, on the professed search for the Positivist conception of things, picks up something else that lies nearer at hand, dubs it "Positivism," and launches it on the stream of controversy. This irrelevance is almost inevitable in a discourse, composed, as it were, to order, without real knowledge of the subject.

The functions of organic elements are directed to the *maintenance* of the organism in the existing state, and only afterwards to the growth from that state to another. Similarly, the social * functions of human beings are directed, first to the maintenance of the existing order of society, and only afterwards to its progress towards any new order. "Order and progress are the watchwords," said Comte.

Now there are four distinct ways in which human beings can contribute to the existing order of society. In the first place it is evident that the existence of the social organism is impossible without the existence of its individual elements. Every individual therefore, by the mere fact of his existence, contributes an essential, though infinitesimal element to the mighty existence including him. Whatever he does moreover to maintain alive other per-

* Properly speaking it is superfluous to add the term "social" to the functions of human beings, since, as we have seen, function for them, necessarily implies relation to society. We have permitted the inaccuracy, precisely for the purpose of emphasizing the fact that it is one.

sons, tends in this same direction. Existence, as we have already said, being the highest conceivable necessity, the multiplication of the existences is always a good, until indeed, by excess, it may come to interfere with the development or well being of those previously created. Here the desirability of existence as multiplied in extension, is checked by the same desirability multiplied in *intension*. It is in this sense that the remark holds true, "whoever makes two blades of grass grow, where only one grew before, is a benefactor to humanity." Finally, the multiplication of existence in *intension*, that is the development and embellishment of individual existences already established, constitute a simple modification of the same function.

The second, and also very obvious way in which human beings contribute to the maintenance of society, is by reproduction. This has always been recognized, and yet, so powerful are the personal and egotistic * passions involved in the birth and in the possession of children, that the recognition is constantly receding into the back ground. Over and over again have state, and church, and public opinion defined the bearing and rearing of children as a social duty, and endeavored, when necessary to enforce it as such. And, over and over again, have either selfish gratification or selfish indifference claimed the right to appropriate or to abandon children, as exclusive per-

* We use this term in no invidious sense, but in the scientific sense of opposition to "altruistic."

sonal property, with which the state could have nothing to do. According to the Positivist conception, which considers reproduction as at once the fulfilment of a profound personal need and as the establishment of an essential organic relation, the rearing of children is ennobled far beyond the scope of the most legitimate and tender personal passion.

It does not enter into our purpose to show how profoundly the birth and the education of children, and the ambitions entertained for them, must be modified by the habit of looking at their possession as a trust held in the service of humanity, trusts whose principal effects are to be felt after the death of the person discharging it. We merely signalize this influence.

The third way in which the human elements can fulfil their functions is by performing some duty recognized as constituting a service for society, and necessitating exertions over and above what may be required for personal maintenance. This involves the whole class of action known as "disinterested" and also the "spirit of disinterestedness" which is recognized as enabling the performance of many fixed duties regarded in themselves as personal occupations. It is the addition of an undefined amount of disinterestedness to strictly necessary exertion, which confers such prestige upon the professions, and also upon public office.* Now in reality,

* "It is assumed," remarks Ruskin, "that a soldier will always be ready to die rather than desert his post; and a physician, rather than desert his patient; and a lawyer rather than betray his client; and a clergyman, rather than forswear the truth."

both the term and the prestige imply a very narrow and incorrect view of what constitutes personal advantage or interest. Taken in an adequate sense, all is of interest to a person that can be made to appear to him interesting. His primary need, is exercise of faculties ; whatever therefore stimulates and facilitates this exercise is in itself an immense advantage, one in fact that must always be implied in any other of the vulgarly recognized advantages, money and fame. The latter is indeed a primary good in itself, but almost inevitably acts by stimulating an extension or repetition of the exertions by which it was originally secured. But money is evidently of use only as it can employ facilities in its expenditure, a remark which is a truism. To sacrifice rewards of money therefore in order to attain some wider satisfaction or " internal reward," is simply to treat it in the only way in which it could be possibly utilized in the attainment of satisfaction. What Catholicism applauds as a matter of heroism, Positivism often approves as a matter of common sense. The vow of poverty, like the resolution of probity, may be common to both ; but the positive method certainly facilitates the diffusion and triumph of a virtue which it plants so firmly on the earth ; while Catholicism increases the difficulties in the way of what it suspends upon the distant heavens. In an artistic sense, as Mr. Mallock would say, this method may sometimes appear more interesting ; except indeed to those who may have suffered real loss by its failure.

To the scholar therefore, the philanthropist, the statesman, even to the physician, the soldier, the teacher, the lawyer, the priest, Mr. Mallock would accord the possibility of conscious joy in the discharge of honorable functions, necessary to the existence of society. But the shoemaker, the butcher, the weaver, the farmer, the servant, can be expected to see no horizon beyond the wall of the little cell in which each lives, and in which the tedium and monotony of his occupation may well lead him to ask, "Is life worth living?"

But a fourth way is now open for these, the great masses of human beings, to complete their lives by the consciousness of a social function. All real occupations must constitute functions in the social organism, for they minister to the real needs of some of its members. Even the practice of personal virtues involves this social relation, because it raises the efficiency of the person practising them. "Thus," says Comte, "even the habit of personal cleanliness becomes elevated from the rank of a simple hygienic precept, by the recollection that it renders each better adapted to serve the others." *

It is no sentimentalism, but the simple expression of fact that the individual occupations of the different mem bers of society, cannot be adequately regulated so long

* This example, however, itself shows very clearly, that the personal virtues are objects of desire in themselves from the development of appropriate tastes for them, and that their value is not defined exclusively by their use. Here, as everywhere in the region of morals, we encounter the double current of æsthetics and utilitarianism; the values which must be *proved*, and the values which must be *recognized*.

as they are regarded merely as the means for each of these persons to get his or her living.

By a crowd of official acts, from the inspection of markets to taking the census, society, "even as it is," expresses its recognition of the fact that this vast mass of activities constituting the "business" of the community, represents the sum of its own vegetative functions, by which all its life, from the lowest to the highest plane of it, is sustained. That in the discharge of these functions the money or "living" earned by each individual is really the least important consideration. Thus, it is of much less importance that a butcher grow rich, than that the thirty or forty families he supplies with meat receive good meat at fair prices. Whatever value attaches to the individual life of the butcher, is multiplied forty times by the sum of those of his customers: it is, therefore, their welfare and not his profit which must be the first consideration. Or, in other words, the essential thing is that meat should be supplied,—the how and the whence are secondary details, to be regulated, not by the convenience of the producer but by that of the consumers.

By this simple but indisputable line of reasoning Positivism, in its study of the laws of social relations. accomplishes two things. In the first place it overturns the theory that work is performed for the sake of the individual, whose advantage indeed is quite subsidiary, and shows that it is primarily for the benefit of society or some group of persons in it. The daily business is thus removed from the ignominy and pettiness of isolated individualism and elevated into an honorable function, while he who performs it becomes invested with the dignity of a public functionary. In the second place, since the welfare of the persons for whom the work is done is the principal thing, and that of the worker secondary to it,* we find at once laid the natural basis for integrity in work, which constitutes indeed one of the principal bases of Positive morality. That the worker receive remuneration is necessary, but an incidental necessity only; that the work be well, thoroughly, honestly done, is so essential that it is inseparable from any typical conception of achievement. By means of work man takes his place among the creative forces of the universe. His work is inevitably liable to the same causes of failure as mar the completeness of other created things; failures due to inadequate conception, deficient vitality, unfavorable medium, hostile forces, blighted growth. But deliberate dishonesty and carelessness is peculiar to human work alone; it is as profoundly unnatural as it is antisocial; it is condemned alike in the world of matter and in the [organic] world of mind.

Thus the Positive workman enjoys to the full the same motive for conscientiousness that Mr. Ruskin celebrates in his mediæval workingmen, at that mythical

* Of course this worker, by entering into another group, where he is the consumer, finds his own welfare correlatively taken into account.

period when "all England awoke every morning and went to its daily work with a prayer." * While the absence of such integrity is a most conspicuous fact in the operations of modern industry, it is none the less certain that the principles of Positivism are logically directed towards the cultivation of a most acute sense of honor in regard to them,—principles now prevailing so little because true Positivism is as yet so little understood. It is true that Catholicism also condemns cheating, and commends the

> "Servant who with this clause
> Makes drudgery divine,
> Who sweeps a room as by God's laws,
> Makes that and the action fine."

But the distinction established between secular and religious duties, cannot fail to weaken the influence of the Church over the duties stamped as inferior. Whereas Positivism, transferring the sense of spirituality to secular duties, welds into one all moral forces for their direction that hitherto have been dispersed.

From what precedes, it is evident that we use the term "occupation" in a double sense. We have already spoken of the need of occupation or action as an elementary need, so essential to the life of a human being as to be strictly analogous to the physical nutriment so essential to the life of his body.† We have also said that

---

* Fors Clavigera.

† This thesis might be developed at great length, even more than has already been done by other writers.

an elementary field for activity was, normally, afforded to every one by the necessity of procuring food or of "getting a living." It may now seem as if we declared that this occupation was itself a function, although elsewhere we have described function as being more exalted in character.

The identity, however, is only apparent. Even when the technical business of a man, whose remuneration is his means of support, occupies all his time, there remains a surplus of activity, which may be directed from the occupation to the function. In the most rudimentary cases this surplus consists entirely of the thoughts and feelings with which the work is regarded by the workman. A thought is as decidedly an expression of human activity as is a piece of handiwork. It is possible that the thought about work shall be merely such as is needed for carrying it on, and of securing some personal advantage from it for the worker. In this case it remains, as far as his consciousness is concerned, only an element of personal nutrition. Or he may regard its performance as it really is, if useful work, namely, as the discharge of a function of society. He may then, for all but the lowest work,* indefinitely increase the expenditure of energy, ingenuity and painstaking bestowed upon it, thus increasing at once the efficiency of the work for the social welfare, and its area as a dwelling-place for his own thoughts.

* Such routine, manual labor as machinery should remove altogether from human hands.

All that has been said of the discharge of functions for the maintenance of social order, applies *cæteris paribus* to such modification of function as may be required in the furtherance of social progress.

Progress may be considered in two aspects. There is the vast and slow progress of the social organism as a whole, and which is principally effected by the élite of humanity—constantly engaged in the discovery of new laws and in the creation of new ideals. The masses contribute to this principally by openheartedness towards new truth, and by loyal seconding of the efforts of their natural leaders. But progress may also be perceived in the developments of individual lives, which, on however small a scale, offer a field for the activity of creative impulse. Whoever freely shapes his life and circumstances according to distinct purposes, that have been tested by the moral and social law and found legitimate, contributes towards the incessant *re*-creation of the social organism through some of its elements; he is an artist in life, greater or smaller according to the scope of his originality, but in any case truly an artist.

In the foregoing exposition we have said nothing of the sentiment of Altruism which is known to occupy a large place in the Positivist social policy. Mr. Mallock does not refer to this sentiment under its technical name, but under other names he is continually falling foul of it, as it were, and accusing it of the consequences of his own misconception. Thus, as we have seen, he tells us that Positivism thinks that "all mankind are made a mighty whole by the fusing power of benevolence. Benevolence, however, means simply the wishing that our neighbors were happy, the helping to make them so, and lastly the being glad that they are so." (p. 69.)* But Positivism says on the contrary that mankind *is* a mighty whole, and that a certain portion of it—the European, with its expansions—have risen into an organic unity through an internal principle of growth.† These are facts of existence and quite independent of the thoughts or feelings that may be entertained about them. Thus, the common destiny and thence the organic unity of Europe was a fact, even when every European nation looked at every other as its natural and permanent enemy. In the same way the organic relations of human beings persist, whether through sentiments of friendship and benevolence these relations occasion a lively happiness, or whether by the influence of egotism and hate, they become a permanent source of pain. Organic relations which have once originated life, are necessarily indissoluble.‡ Stated less technically, the assertion of Positivism is that the dependence of the spiritual life of one man upon others is demonstrated practically by the fact that the immense majority of his thoughts and feelings are directed towards these others;

---

* See remainder of quotation as given on p. 20.

† See Appendix

‡ Thus no growth of hatred can really dissolve the union by which the lives of two human beings have become fused into that of offspring. This is why Comte so fully endorsed the Catholic doctrine on the indissolubility of marriage.

whether these feelings be amiable or unamiable. And theoretically the same fact is explained by the doctrine of the social organism, which shows how the real isolation of elements is impossible. Thus, the man who betrays a trust in order to secure a fortune, can spend but little of this in physical, sensuous and æsthetic enjoyments; the greater portion must go towards securing prestige, consideration, applause, companionship of human beings similar to those whom he may have ruined, and whose sentiments of consideration cannot be more than an equivalent for the sentiments of confidence he has forfeited. Moreover, this forfeiture has not annihilated social relations even with this group of persons, but has established them upon undying sentiments of hate and distrust. In trying, therefore, to escape from human beings, he finds himself permanently, inevitably confronted by humanity.

Anti-social conduct does not represent a reality, but a desire, and a tendency, which can only be realized by death. All injury of human beings expresses a tendency which points steadily towards their murder: for it expresses a more or less intense desire to rupture relations, which nevertheless cannot be ruptured but only changed as long as the persons between whom they have been established remain alive.* Thus, long ago it was said, "Whosoever hateth his brother is a murderer." It is

*Thus there is a sense in which De Quincey's paradoxical advice,—not to begin with murder lest it might lead to incivility,—ceases to be a paradox.

this sense of the indissolubility, in some form or another of human relations, which constitutes the essence of the sentiment of Altruism. It is not a mere sentimentality, but a strict deduction from a scientific theory of life.

The sentiment of benevolence is not the foundation of Altruism, but is deduced from it. It begins ultimately in the reflection that since our lives are so inseparably united it is reasonable to make the union a source of pleasure instead of suffering. This reflection having originated certain actions which tend to repeat themselves, the emotion is generated, according to the general psychological law, that the constant repetition of the same thoughts or actions is invariably attended by the generation of a sentiment appropriate to them, and which grows more intense with every repetition of the actions. Similarly with the sentiments of justice, of compassion, of sympathy,* of tenderness, etc. These all ultimately depend on the more or less conscious appreciation of a community in nature and destiny between the persons entertaining these sentiments and those in whose behalf they are entertained.† They have therefore the most profound basis possible, not "resting on a pedestal,"

---

* In the narrower sense.

† In the abstract line of reasoning we are pursuing, we may not pause for concrete illustrations. But we have often pondered on one historical fact which most curiously demonstrates the influence of supposed community of destiny on the sentiments of justice and compassion. This fact is that the practice of infanticide as an acknowledged right, so long survived the practice, at first co-existent with it, of murder of aged and infirm parents. The reason is, that the homicides learned to look forward to the day when they also should be old, but always knew that they never again could be babies.

but rooting themselves in the primary conditions of existence.

Before proceeding to show how the questions of morality and of the prize of life are to be solved in accordance with the positive conceptions of Altruism and of the Social Organism, we must return for a moment to our starting-point. It will be remembered that, among Mr. Mallock's readers, we claimed to especially address ourselves to those who were liable to be attracted to Catholicism by its promises of unity, certainty, authority, and mighty communion. We asserted that, however successfully in the past Catholicism had fulfilled these promises, in the present day Positive thought was really alone capable of doing so. Let us compare the two in their principal details :

"The primary doctrine of the church," says Mr. Mallock, "is her own perpetual infallibility. * * * The Church of Rome essentially is the spiritual sense of humanity speaking to men through its proper and only possible organ. * * * The church, it is undeniable, has for a long time lived and moved amongst countless false opinions ; and to the external age they have naturally seemed a part of her. But science (!) moves on, and it is shown that she can cast them off. It may absorb ideas that we should consider broader, bolder, and more natural than any it seems to possess at present. * * * The church is a living organism, still full of vigor and power of self-adaptation, and will be able to develop as the world develops around her, and yet lose nothing of her supernatural sameness."

If for the unmeaning clause, "supernatural sameness," we substitute the words "permanent identity," we shall find in the above a real description of the far greater "living organism" of humanity. Humanity is infallible, not in the sense of never having fallen into error, but as being the only conceivable source of truth. For what truth can be named or was ever known that did not emanate from a human breast and brain? The "proper and only possible organ" through which "the spiritual sense of humanity can speak to men," is the voice of man himself. For, from the moment that argument has once been thought necessary, what argument has ever demonstrated a radical difference between the natures of the speakers standing in the line of apostolic succession and those outside of it? It is the message which tests the worth of the speaker, and not the reverse. And it is preëminently true of humanity that it is an organism "full of vigor and power of self-adaptation," with indefinite possibilities of expansion and development.

What comfort is to be derived from the sense of membership in the church that is not to be found in the sense of membership in humanity, when that is once really understood? How does the communion of technical saints differ in essence or in sweetness from the communion of *all* the righteous? Why should the church militant for the propagation of an artifical theology or the aggrandisement of an anonymous priesthood awaken more enthusiasm than human heroism militant against tyrannies and wrong and oppression and suffering? Is this "grace and mercy which comes through the set channels" of the parish priest of the neighborhood any more precious than that which reaches us by the natural channels of gracious and merciful human beings wherever found?

To the Catholic, the priesthood is the appointed organ of Providence, the special medium for the goodness of God. To the Positivist, for whom the designs of Providence are identified with the will of humanity, all goodness is divine, and known not only in that which he may receive, but in that of which he may himself be the author. It is no assertion of modern "materialism" when a man, flushed with the glow of generous action or a great thought, declares himself to be the instrument of God. Positive thought, far from condemning this audacity, applauds it as the literal expression of the truth. It does more; for into the heart of him who is discouraged by waiting for the slow purpose of Providence to be revealed, it breathes the suggestion: Be your own providence; create your own good. All the good that ever came into the world came through some man of like nature with yourself. Why not then through you? Renew in your own person the eternal mystery of the incarnation, of the descent of divine truth in the flesh among men!'

It is difficult to see how this conception of the position of man is less dignified than that he held under the old theology. Yet Mr. Mallock's first, second and last accusation against Positivism is that it deprives man of all the pathetic dignity which he had acquired by Christianity. "Under the light of [its] conceptions man appeared an ampler being. His thoughts were forever being gazed upon by the controller of all things; he was made in the likeness of the Lord of lords; he was akin to the power before which all the visible world trembled; and every detail in the life of the human soul became vaster beyond all comparison than the depths of space and time." (p. 21.)

We might notice in passing, that whoever has been in the habit of considering space and time as categories or conditions of human thought, would not find this last comparison of any especial significance. But this is by the way. It cannot of course be denied, and Positivists would be the last to question, that the glory belonging to man as the lowest of the angels, may be amplified to the imagination, as well as that of being the real lord of creation.* Indeed there are few conceptions of the human intelligence which are not susceptible of being glorified by the human imagination,—the wife of the understanding. But who goes to a man's wife to learn how he stands in business, or what is his real rank in science? This is the fatal error which vitiates all Mr. Mallock's eloquence; he relies on it not only to adorn but to support. To use

* Comte observes somewhere, "This is looking at man as the first of the animals, instead of as the lowest of the angels."

one of his own illustrations slightly altered: "If my friend says such a view of things is beautiful and noble and inspiring, and I find myself inspired by the exact opposite, how shall I prove that my state of mind is more rational than his?" For a state of imagination cannot be either rational or irrational. The question is whether the objects which occasion it are real or fantastic; whether the scheme of thought which it clothes is true or untrue.

This test we have seen Mr. Mallock deliberately rejects, and we shall have occasion in a few moments to discuss seriously the theory of his rejection. But at this moment we would prefer to call attention to an internal inconsistency in the conception whose dignity he invokes,—inconsistency which has had serious practical consequences.

No one can know better than Mr. Mallock that the belief that the "thoughts of man were constantly being gazed upon by the great controller of all things," is a belief which has served quite as often to crush as to inspire. He himself, when he sees it in the interest of another line of argument, holds out as an inducement to the Catholic theology, that by it "man's nature will be redeemed visibly from its weakness and its littleness." He cannot but know that, except to pure Deism, the correlative of the belief in question has always been the absolute worthlessness, wickedness and ruined condition of man; has been a theory of the complete degradation of every faculty and impulse of his nature; so much so that his eternal salvation depended on his denying and mortifying this nature, and that every natural crisis of his earthly career, from birth to death, must be looked upon as exposing to the deadliest dangers until they had been redeemed by a sacrament of the Church. We must never forget that, in Mr. Mallock's view at least, the simple conception of Theism is only like "an alluring voice, heard far off through a fog, and calling 'Follow me,' only to leave its followers to be killed or crippled among rocks and streams and pitfalls." (p. 266.) While the Christian or Catholic conception, whose introduction into the world is alleged as conferring such an immense increase of human dignity, has, indisputably, been attended by conceptions of human vileness, perhaps more intense than have ever existed anywhere except in Hindustan.

There is however a sense in which the assertion is true, "that man became an ampler being in the light of this conception." Against this native vileness and natural tendency to perdition, were to be contrasted the salvation and hope of glory which had been procured for him at the expense of a stupendous celestial drama, enacted for his benefit ages before he came into existence. The contemplation of this imaginary scheme of salvation, the task of connecting with it an innumerable mass of details of daily life, have unquestionably occupied thousands, perhaps millions of minds, in a way to greatly enlarge to their appreciation, the sense of the importance of their own lives, for which so much pains had been expended. But after all, the sense of glowing gratitude for redemption, which has certainly ravished the heart of many a saint, cannot more than balance the terrors of perdition. The note of praise and the note of despair combine in the concerto executed by skilful musicians. When they cease to play, despair and praise vanish together.*

Again: Catholicism has often been praised, and justly, for its intervention in favor of the weak things of this world and the despised, whom it lifted upon a plane with the strong on account of the equality of both before the tribunal for eternal salvation. Catholicism is thus celebrated as the liberator of the slave, as the emancipator of women, as the succor of the poor, the sick, and the oppressed,—and, we repeat, with justice. But it is just also to notice that this liberation was not effected by bestowing strength upon weakness, but by placing weakness on a forced equality with strength. Above all virtues the church has cultivated those of humility and obedience, and these are naturally more easy to cultivate in the weak than in the strong,—hence the weak received at once a hitherto unparalleled consideration. If the human rights of a slave could only be secured after protection had been obtained for him as a member of the church; and if the intrinsic worth of human nature could only be recognized after it had been stamped as worthless, then

* As Defoe long ago remarked as an excuse for writing a "History of the Devil:" "For it is generally observed that those who cease to believe in the Devil soon disbelieve in God also."

on the whole humanity has gained by the inconsistency.*
But our line of argument will not permit us to forget the abject degradation of thought and life which, as most logical consequence of its cardinal doctrines of human nature, marked the period of complete ascendency of the church. Whatever in the middle ages was great, or rich, or strong, or beautiful, was obtained in spite of these doctrines. It was conflict with them which nourished the most robust virtues; it was forgetfulness of them that permitted the first growth of art; it was defiance of them which hewed out the first steps of science. And these are the doctrines which, we are now told, can alone save the dignity of man, menaced by the ravages of Positivism. Mr. Mallock strikes his key-note falsely. He decks mediæval Catholicism in the transparent robes of modern Unitarian optimism, and expects the anachronism to pass undetected. He forgets that the "focalization of the diffused light of the supernatural" has often served merely to efface the natural sunshine in its lurid glare!

It is characteristic of nearly all modern theistic discussions on the doctrine of a future life, that this is assumed to be a doctrine of invariable comfort and promise. The reverse of the medal is kept out of sight. Now, the sermons against "infidels" of the seventeenth and eighteenth centuries assume, on the contrary, that this doctrine of a

* Although it is not for *this* generation to forget that the chains which the Spanish church forged for the negro in the interest of the Indian, were afterwards padlocked by the American church in the interest of commerce.

future life is a terrible one. There are so many more people to be lost than there are to be saved, that the prospect of immortality cannot fail to cast a huge shadow over all mortal existence. Then "infidels" were warned not to "lull themselves in fancied security," not to enjoy life too much, since they could not tell what might be in store for them, which, in a short time, would more than prevent them from enjoying at all. But to-day the adjuration is made, as if the anticipation of immortality were the only thing that lent value to mortality, and gave the hope which alone could make "life worth living."

Mr. Mallock, in making this adjuration, passes in the most airy manner possible over the "difficulties" once felt in the way of responding to it. As to the second question,—that of eternal punishment—he remarks "we may certainly here *get rid of one difficulty** by adopting the doctrine of a final restitution." (p. 255). But it certainly never occurred to either Bossuet or Massillon, either to Jeremy Taylor or to Richard Baxter, that "difficulties" could be thus bowled out of the way as easily as billiard balls, merely by "adopting" some other view of them. For they would have believed that they dishonored their cause if they once admitted, as Mr. Mallock does, that "reason and observation" justify the position of the obdurates whom they were trying to summon to salvation. (p. 254.) "If we believe in heaven, we believe in something the imagination fails to grasp. If we be-

* Italics ours.

lieve in hell, we believe in something the imagination revolts at. * * * From these difficulties it is impossible to escape. * * * We can only show that they are inevitable, not that they are not insoluble. If we condemn a belief in heaven because it is unthinkable, we must for the same reason condemn a Utopia upon earth." (p. 254–255.)

This doctrine of what we have already called "equivalent inexplicablenesses," is so important for Mr. Mallock's purposes that we may not longer delay a formal examition of it. This examination will lead us away from the climax of Catholicism into which we have followed Mr. Mallock's reasoning, into the devious ways of that reasoning itself. With it, therefore, we may very properly open the third and last portion of our review.

III.

Stated simply, we might almost say, brutally, the doctrine of equivalent inexplicableness runs thus: "Here is something that I cannot explain, but you cannot explain it either. Therefore when I assert something else that I still am not able to explain, you can say nothing against it."

This is the gist of Mr. Mallock's chapter on "Morality and Natural Theism," which is headed by the too famous motto, "credo quia impossibile est."

Mr. Mallock wishes to discuss the "moral objections" that have been brought against the Catholic conception of God. To obtain a concrete and forcible presentation of these objections, he quotes from James Mill, what he calls "the vulgar view of the matter." "Mr. Mill" says his son, "looked upon religion as the greatest enemy of morality; first, by setting up fictitious excellences; * * * but above all by radically vitiating the standard of morals, making it consist in doing the will of a being, on whom indeed it lavishes all the praises of adulation, but whom in sober truth, it depicts as eminently hateful. I have a hundred times heard him say that all ages and nations have represented their gods as wicked in a constantly increasing progression: * * * but the *ne plus ultra* of wickedness he considered to be embodied in what is commonly presented to mankind as the creed of Christianity. Think, (he used to say), of a being who would make a hell, who would create the human race with the infallible fore-knowledge, and therefore with the intention that the great majority of them should be consigned to horrible and everlasting torment." Mr. Mallock considers that this way of putting things is "vulgar," and contains a great deal of "coarse and exaggerated acrimony." In order to refine the matter sufficiently to be brought within reach of his own delicate handling, he sums up Mr. Mill's position thus: "His main difficulty is nothing more than this: How can an infinite will that rules everywhere, find room for a finite will not in harmony with itself? Whilst the only further perplexity (!) that the passage indicates, is the existence of those evil conditions by which the finite will, already so weak and wavering is yet further hampered." (p. 251.)

By this euphemistic translation of Mr. Mill's more vigorous language, Mr. Mallock believes that he has accomplished a great feat; he has shown that these are "not moral difficulties at all, but *merely** intellectual difficulties." (p. 251.)

The naïveté of this assertion is astonishing. "*Merely* intellectual difficulties!" How could our author speak more contemptuously of the human intelligence if he had

* Italics ours.

imitated the wicked Positivists and reduced it to a lump of clay? And do "moral difficulties" involve no questions of thought? Are questions of morals nothing but ripples of feeling?

However it may be, Mr. Mallock is evidently convinced that by this single assertion he has disposed of the whole matter in admitting that the theology in question "involves a contradiction in terms." (p. 251.) He continues in the next paragraph to observe that "theology accepts it [this contradiction], with its eyes wide open, making no attempt to explain the inexplicable; and the human will it treats in the same way" [*i. e.*, as the doctrine of eternal damnation]. "It makes no offer to us to clear up everything, or to enable thought to put a girdle round universe. On the contrary, it proclaims with emphasis that its first axioms are unthinkable, and its most renowned philosophic (?) motto is, 'I believe because it is impossible.'"

The logical consequence of this position should be, as we should imagine, that the theologian would peremptorily decline all controversy, which must be carried on in thinkable terms, under pain of degenerating into gibberish. But, as is well known, theology has never been in the habit of declining controversy, and perhaps for that very reason, has not always avoided the penalty in question.

Still less does Mr. Mallock, theologian, lined or veneered with a philosopher, decline controversy or elaborate thinking in terms which he announces as "unthinkable." He is like a man in a wrestling match, ignorant of the principles of the art of wrestling, but who has learned a special trick by which he confidently expects to *throw* his antagonist. This trick is an *et tu quoque.* "It" (theology) "will not deny its own condition, but it will show his opponent that his is really the same. * * * If good be a thing of any spiritual value, if it be, in other words, what every moral system supposes it to be, that good can co-exist with evil is just as unthinkable as that God can," etc. (p. 252.)

The "mysteries" which Mr. Mallock signalizes as off-setting all the doctrines of the church, are the freedom of will, the connection of consciousness with the brain, the interference of volition with the uniform course of nature. We will consider these topics in their place. But in this place we must return to the principle in whose support they are brought forward.

The principle rests on a double confusion: first a confusion between facts and theories, and then a confusion between assumed and indubitable facts.

Now, in regard to the first: Our inability to explain a fact cannot throw the least doubt upon its existence, if this has been testified to us in the legitimate way; but the inability of a theory to satisfactorily explain the fact to which it relates, or without contradiction of other facts equally well attested, or by necessitating the existence of facts not well attested at all, such inability, we say, is sufficient reason for rejection of the theory.

Thus the existence of the spleen is a fact, whose existence is attested by our senses in the most indubitable manner. But the theory of the function of a spleen which attributes to it the manufacture of a "cold and peccant humor," necessitates the demonstration to the senses of the existence of such a fluid—demonstration which has not and never can be furnished. Hence the theory falls to the ground. But no perfectly satisfactory theory has yet been suggested to take its place: hence, provisionally, we remain in doubt about some of the functions of the spleen. Yet this doubt cannot invalidate by one tittle the fact of the spleen's existence.

Again, facts are indubitable, either when they are themselves the direct objects of mental perception or of the activity of some of the senses,* or when, by a simple or complex series of equivalents, they can be brought into relation with that perception or with those senses. Thus the emotion of anger is a real fact, be-because directly perceived in consciousness; and the stomach is a real fact, because, under certain circumstances, it can be seen and handled. Again, injustice is a complex real fact, one of whose equivalents, or one chain in the link connecting it with consciousness, is the emotion of anger it excites. And the digestion of food by the stomach is a real fact, although it becomes known

* See pp. 61 and 72.

only by means of a long series of intermediate facts or impressions made on the senses, not one of which alone would suffice to suggest it.

Thus, in regard to *material* facts, Mr. Mallock is quite right when he says that they are only supposed to be proved, "when, directly or indirectly, their material equivalent can be impressed upon our bodily senses." (p. 214.) But he is quite wrong, and quite disingenuous, moreover, when he pretends that the only facts known to Positivists are of this description. Of this more anon.

All facts, claiming to be such, but not answering to the above definitions, are assumed facts. Assumption of fact is often legitimate, but only on one condition. The assumption must either be permanently maintained as such, as in the region of professed imagination; or else it must constitute a provisional hypothesis, adopted in explanation of some real fact, and which may be abandoned either if it fails to explain or it fails itself to be verified in the usual manner. Even when it affords a satisfactory explanation, it cannot be fully accepted, *i. e.*, the mind cannot repose on it as true until this external verification has been obtained. To say otherwise would be to return at once to the antique test of truth, internal harmony and consistency.* On the other hand, if the assumed facts do not explain but rather contradict the undoubted fact, all ground for the assumption is taken away.

Thus, in a word, failure to explain a fact cannot in-

* See p. 73.

validate a fact, and an assumed fact that is inexplicable or contradictory or useless, cannot be compared with a real fact that has not been explained. Concerning a real fact, we are not obliged to ask about its utility; but the utility of an assumed fact is its only excuse for being.

But Mr. Mallock's proposition is: There are certain facts that, on their own showing, the Positivists cannot explain. Therefore they have not the shadow of a right to object when we assume a few facts that we are quite ready to admit are inexplicable and contradictory. We do it with our eyes wide open.

Thus: "If good be a thing of any spiritual value, that good can coexist with evil is just as unthinkable as that God can." (p. 252.) Let us transpose a little. It is a fact, perceptible to every one so as to admit of no dispute, that good and evil are found coexisting in the universe. But "good" is something of spiritual value. Therefore it is impossible to conceive of such coexistence of good and evil—it is unthinkable. It is also impossible to conceive of God coexisting with evil. But as we have just been forced to admit one impossibility, there is no reason why we should not admit two. Therefore we do admit two impossibilities.

If it were not for the gravity of the subject, we could not refrain from remarking that this reason for a second "admission" suggests the reasons sometimes urged in favor of drinking a second bottle. It certainly seems to lead to a mental condition the reverse of "truth and soberness."

A *fact* is never "unthinkable." The coexistence of good and evil in this world is a fact, attested by such manifold evidence that it cannot be doubted. That "good" is a "spiritual thing" emanating from a personal God, who, though omnipotent and with infinite detestation of evil, permits its continuance,—this is not a fact, but the statement of a theory to explain the real fact, *i. e.*, the coexistence of good and evil. There is not, therefore, the least parallelism between the two statements. As moreover the second statement, or the theory, far from explaining the fact, enshrouds it in much greater mystery than it naturally possessed, we are left without any inducement to take this theory into consideration.

Again: "Free will," says Mr. Mallock, "is a moral necessity: [but] it is an intellectual impossibility: [nevertheless] though it be impossible, we yet, in defiance of intellect, continue as moral beings to believe in it. Let us but once realize that we do this, that all mankind universally do this and have done it, and the difficulties offered us by Theism will no longer stagger us. * * * If in spite of my reason I can believe that my will is free,—in spite of my reason I can believe that God is good." (p. 260.) And again we say: It is absurd for a person who announces his intention of "defying reason" with all the hardihood of a moral Ajax, to attempt to *reason* with the public and to show persuasive reasons for saying, "I believe though it is impossible."

Deferring for a moment the real consideration of these "difficulties," let us here confine our attention to one point only, namely, the reason alleged by Mr. Mallock for referring in this place to the Freedom of the Will. This reason is that as it is a fact of consciousness, and yet unintelligible, unintelligibility constitutes no reason for rejecting credence in any alleged fact whatever. The syllogism runs thus:

The Freedom of the Will is unintelligible.

$(x=y)$.

The moral attributes of God are unintelligible.

$(z=y)$.

But the Freedom of the Will is a fact of human consciousness.

$(x=u)$.

Therefore the moral attributes of God as described in theology are facts external to human consciousness.

$(z=v)$

Here is a double fallacy. In the first place the middle term is not distributed, and it does not follow, though any particular number of facts were unintelligible, that conversely, anything unintelligible could be assumed to be a matter of fact; and in the second place the term "fact" is used ambiguously, and in a way to imply either an internal fact of consciousness, or a fact of the world external to consciousness. If any conclusion could be drawn from this reasoning it would be that the theological assertion of the moral attributes of God was exclusively a fact of human consciousness. This is indeed the only correct conclusion, but it is categorically opposed to the external reality, which we are told at the outset, is to be established. But, as seen by the rules of logic, no conclusion could be drawn. Nor could it even if we give the implied extension to the true fact and said, "The Freedom of the Will, though a fact, is unintelligible."

($x=u$), and

Therefore the moral attributes of God, which are also unintelligible, are facts.

($z=u$).

For to draw this conclusion we should have to introduce a clause containing the particular term (unintelligible) enlarged to a universal, thus;

All unintelligible things are facts.

($u=y$).

Freedom of the will and the moral attributes of God are facts.

(x and $z=y$).

But we think even Mr. Mallock's hardihood would recoil before this necessary clause.

Therefore, even though it should be true that the Freedom of the Will were a fact so difficult of comprehension as to be called "unintelligible," the existence of such a fact would not offer the slightest warrant for any theological mysteries whatever. And that, first, because it has nothing to do with them, and "unintelligibility" is no common ground for inference. Second, because if a fact, it is a fact of internal consciousness, and therefore not to be paralleled with facts external to consciousness.*

In reality, however, as we have already seen, it is impossible that a fact should be unintelligible, even when its origin and relations are temporarily or permanently inexplicable. The coexistence of evil and good, the freedom of the will, the connection of consciousness with the brain, the disturbance of uniformities of nature by human volition, least of all the Positivist's "Utopia," are all subjects involving problems of varying degrees of difficulty, but which, in so far as they involve facts, are not unintelligible at all.

But what perception of consciousness, or what impression on the senses, or what reliable testimony demonstrates the reality of the "Hell at which our moral sense revolts," and of the omnipotent yet powerless Person who, from all eternity, watches myriads of sentient beings falling into it, like flies into a Gehenna of molasses?

Mr. Mallock does not pretend to adduce any. He merely asserts that this doctrine, though disagreeable, is inseparably bound up with other doctrines so agreeable and so comforting, that we could not possibly wish to reject them.

And it is in regard to these *assumed* facts that he brings forward his famous doctrine, "Proof is not necessary for

* See p. 61.

the establishment of truth." Now we have already seen * that for the acceptance of internal ideals, the creation of consciousness, external proof was *not* necessary. It always is desirable to establish a real corelation between the internal ideal, and the external conditions in the midst of which it has been evolved; but the final reason for an ideal of conduct as of art, lies in itself, and in its internal adaptation to the approval of the human mind. *The transfer of this doctrine from the internal world of consciousness to the world of external facts, where it is no longer in the least applicable, is the central juggle of all Mr. Mallock's reasoning.* "You believe in pure actions; this is the same thing as admitting a substance called Purity, created by a Being living somewhere where he cannot be seen."

To the original mystification caused by the establishment of a false parallelism between facts and theories, and between real and assumed facts, he adds another, caused by an equally false parallelism between internal truth, the *creation* of the mind; and external truth, or the true relations of things external to the mind, and only *perceived* by it.†

Let us now examine in turn, each of these alleged "unintelligibilities." And first, the Freedom of the Will. Mr.

* See page 81.

† By "external to the mind" we of course mean external to the personality of the person perceiving. We leave on one side the profoundly interesting conceptions of idealism, and the question whether these apparently external things do not after all lie *in* the mind.

Mallock touches upon this weighty topic several times in the course of his book. In his chapter on the Logic of Scientific Negation, he denounces the Positivist attempt to reduce man to an automaton, and is particularly severe on the "iron strength of logic" by which he thinks that this has been done. In the same chapter however he appeals to logic, to show that "every exertion of the human will is a miracle in the strictest sense of the word: only it takes place privately within the walls of the brain." (p. 243.) This ingenious suggestion has been borrowed from our American theologian Bushnell.* In an earlier chapter, entitled "Life as its own reward," we are told that "a certain supernatural moral judgment has become a primary faculty with us;" (p. 193) and gives to art, among other things, all its value. But this faculty of moral judgment will be destroyed or paralyzed by Positivism, which intends to reduce man to an automaton, *i. e.*, to deprive him of free will. Because Positivism means to reduce everything to science, and science is only possible when nature is uniform, but "morality is only possible when this uniformity is interfered with by the will." (p. 246.)

And this antithesis between science and morality is repeated in the sentence we have now recently quoted: "Free will is a moral necessity; it is an intellectual impossibility, [but] though it be impossible we yet, in defiance of intellect, continue as moral beings to believe in it."

* Essay on the Natural and the Supernatural.

(p. 260.) In this last sentence Mr. Mallock undesignedly contradicts the reason previously given for referring to the freedom of the will as an offset to theological mysteries. He then asserted that this was a *fact*, seen to be indubitable the moment any one abandoned speculation and interrogated his own consciousness. He now says on the contrary that it is not a fact which imposes itself on the mind, indeed the mind would not believe in it at all were it not forced to do so by a "moral necessity," *i. e.*, we presume, by conviction that this belief is necessary for the maintenance of morals. To say that we can compel to belief a mind that *cannot* believe, sounds like a claim to be able to make a paralyzed man walk by an alarm of fire. Only hysterical paralysis can be dissipated by such alarms.

The "moral necessity" is that of recognizing persons as responsible for their actions, and able to choose between doing or not doing any particular thing. The "intellectual impossibility" Mr. Mallock does not define; he merely alludes to it as something perfectly well known. We presume, therefore, he means the impossibility of thinking of the determination of the will except in obedience to the strongest motive, and the impossibility in that case of looking at the will as self-determined enough to be free.

In addition to these standard, recognized, and respectable difficulties which Mr. Mallock is, as it were, ready to admit into good company, there are others which he considers merely as inventions of the Positivist, considerations involving the physical conditions of volition, which tend "to reduce man to an automatic part of nature."

Let us apply the Positive method to these two cases.

The "self-determination of the will" is an idea involving all the confusion inherent in the conception of entities. Here is one inside the other, like the boxes in a Chinese puzzle. First there is the soul, an "entity separable from the body." Then there is the Will inside the soul, another entity, absolute and without relations to any thing, not even with other parts of the soul. For to be closely allied with feelings, or tastes, or judgments, would subject the Will to the injurious suspicion of being guided by something instead of being like—it is impossible to think of any other simile for a self-determined will,—some automatic toy which, once wound up, propels itself indefinitely, in unforseeable directions.

What does the interrogation of consciousness really reveal? A continuous succession of ideas and feelings, linked together by more or less close bonds of association, appearing in series more or less habitual, offering weaker or stronger attractions towards practical activities. What events take place, according to our consciousness, when we decide in favor of one line of action rather than of another? The motives in favor of this course, perhaps at first repulsed, continue to return to consciousness; gradually establish themselves there to the exclusion of the others opposing, which recede in proportion. When we become exclusively conscious of motives in one direction, retaining of their opposites nothing but an inoperative reminiscence, the decision is already made. Nothing intervenes between our conscious mental desire and its practical realization except the obstacles external to our personality, which we proceed to remove by successive actions. Or, as it might be and has been technically expressed, by successive movements which, in the absence of external hinderance, are the direct result of the state of sensibility known as desire.*

But it will be asked, what is this force, who is this individual who summons or repulses these series of motives? Either he does so voluntarily, in which case alone he is free; or he submits to their influence involuntarily, in which case he is an automaton, devoid of moral responsibility.

In this as in all other cases of conflict between the Positive method and what, by a permissible ellipsis we may call the Catholic, the first essential for a solution of the problem is its restatement, and a definition of terms. What then is an automaton?

Goltz † in the lucid researches, which so well illus-

---

* As for our purpose it is necessary to avoid technicalities as much as possible, we refrain from pursuing the profoundly interesting analysis by which the original reflex arc of sensibility and movement is developed by the interposition of the "accessory sphere" of the intelligence. See p. 69.

† Ueber den Sitz der Seele des Frosches. 1868.

trate the Positive method, defines an automaton to be something whose movements can be submitted to calculation. The movements of a creature possessed of individual will cannot be calculated; they occur spontaneously, without *direct* reference to any external stimulus or suggestion. Indirectly, remotely, such external stimulus may be found; but its influence is experienced in the individual character and habits which may have become determined by it, and not in any specific act.

This difference between voluntary and automatic action is so precise, that it admits of being demonstrated even in so "rudimentary a soul," * as that of a frog. An ordinary frog, kept under observation, will be found at irregular intervals to enter spontaneously into movement, in obedience to impulses of exclusively internal origin. These impulses are in accordance with habits generated by long contact of the frog's organism with a fixed medium; but they are the direct expression only of the spontaneous activity of the organism. If now a certain portion of the brain be removed, (the cerebral hemispheres,) these spontaneous movements cease. An automatic mechanism remains, of such exquisite adjustment, that many complex actions will still be performed in obedience to special stimuli. The frog will rub away a drop of irritating acid from his back, will leap out of the way of an obstacle, etc., but he never takes any initiative of

* We quote Goltz's expression.

action,* and while undisturbed from without remains motionless. This is the essential characteristic of voluntary power or of free will, extending from the lowest animal existence to man. The belief in free will is founded, not as Mr. Mallock crudely supposes, in moral utility, but in a fact of observation as well as of consciousness. Consciousness shows the successive series or "compounds" of ideas and feelings cohering into an individual *I*. Observation shows that as a final result of internal conflict between these ideas and feelings, an action results, which we call spontaneous because no other origin can be found for it than the mental activity of this complex individual. As neither consciousness nor observation reveal the existence of any "self-determining entity" called will, the positive method consigns it to the limbo of other entities, retaining the name as a necessary formula for expressing the parts of volition.

"Yes," cries Mr. Mallock reproachfully, "that is exactly what you *do* do, and hence away with moral responsibility and the moral law, and the struggles of conscience, and the dignity of art, and the beauty of life. No one need do anything but resign himself to the soulless task of passively watching the thoughts and feelings that arise in his own mind, and drifting with their current. No one can blame him for going in any direction, any more than

* Of course it would be inappropriate here to discuss the experiments of Pflüger and Lewes, and their, as we believe unsuccessful, attempt to controvert this position.

one can blame a wretch whose boat is carried over the falls of Niagara." * Observation shows however, that the sense of responsibility is attached to many other things besides volitions. The responsibility for ignorance, in circumstances where knowledge is required, is universally recognized. A physician who, through ignorance and in spite of the best intentions, maltreats a patient, may be sued for malpractice. An engineer who wrecks a train because he has neglected to acquaint himself with the signals, is removed from his position with disgrace. In the innumerable cases where no definite injury of other persons demands the infliction of legal punishment, ignorance continues to draw down fatal vengeance on the heads of well-meaning fools. Life has no pardon for those who are ignorant of the right way of living; nature and society combine to mete out punishment, which is precisely the only method known to the civil law for defining moral responsibility.

Nor for ignorance alone. If the civil law limit itself to the punishment of overt acts, the moral law, as expressive of public opinion, condemns quite as strenuously the wicked feelings which have been the immediate antecedents of the act. Mr. Mallock points out this himself when he insists on the "inwardness" of the moral end. "By calling the moral end inward, I mean that it resides primarily not in action but in motives to action: in the

* For once we do not make a literal quotation, but we certainly express the sense.

will [*i. e.*, desire,] not in the deed ; not in what we actually do, but in what we actually endeavor to do." (p. 88.) Mr. Mallock admits that at least some Positivists would agree with him that "the moral end is a certain inward state of the heart or mind—a state which will of necessity, if possible, express itself in action, but whose value is not to be measured by the success of that expression. The battle-ground of good and evil is within us : and the great human event is the issue of the struggle between them." (p. 89.) Very well put, Mr. Mallock ; but in that case what becomes of the "moral necessity" for believing in a will "free" from the influence of motives ? The moral responsibility is shown to attach, not only to the external action which will result from the final issue of this internal conflict, but to the nature of the motives sustaining it. "Whosoever *hateth* his brother is a murderer : " Although quoting argument from one Positivist, Mr. Mallock insists that Positivism destroys the inwardness of the moral end. He is to be condemned for the feeling of hate which has arisen spontaneously in his consciousness, even though he successfully struggle against the voluntary impulse towards which the feeling directs itself. And if it can be shown that the feeling of hate is the unavoidable result of feelings of suspicion, or envy, or jealousy, the condemnation is not lessened but increased. Still further, although there is a sense in which human compassion intervenes to mitigate the severity of condemnation for acts or characteristics which result from inherited tendencies of organization, or depend upon physical infirmities, the laws of nature (which to the Catholic must be the laws of God) admit of no such mitigation. The man who yields to an inherited impulse to drink, sinks to perdition as fast or faster than one who becomes a drunkard through a vicious taste for low companionship. He whose suspicions and irritable temper come to him as his share in a family tendency to insanity, finishes none the less by embittering his life with needless enemies.

"Nature forgets no debt and fears no grave."

And again we say, it is impossible to distinguish by the results such retribution for organic defects, from the "punishment" inflicted on violated "voluntary" responsibilities.

When we say, therefore, that a human being is responsible for his actions, we mean that he will and must bear the consequences of them. This law of responsibility is innate in the relations of things, and is so much wider and more exact than any which could be devised by a human tribunal, civil or ecclesiastic, that it admits no palliating circumstances, no excuse of ignorance or weakness, except such as may be secured by the intervention of human compassion. "Whatsoever a man soweth *that* shall he also reap."

The mystery—for there is one—does not lie in any "entity" inside of the spiritual individuality of man, but in that individuality itself; in the nexus which coheres into one definite unit, the succession of thoughts and feelings of which we are conscious in ourselves; and into another the succession of actions of which we observe in our neighbor.* In the one case and in the other we are able to trace manifold series of phenomena in constantly converging lines; but the point of convergence escapes us. Yet it is this point of convergence of thoughts, feelings, instincts, habits, physical and mental conditions and tendencies, which constitutes the *I* and the *thou*. The scientific test of freedom, spontaneous activity, applies to the whole of this individuality, and not merely to a part of it. For of the whole it must be said, that however nearly we may approximate, we can never positively calculate on the future direction of that activity—whether of thoughts, or of feelings, or of volitions. It is as easy to foresee how a man will act, as how he will feel, and in neither case is it, with scientific precision, possible. The impossibility depends on the individuality, and not on the spirituality of the individual, as is shown by the fact that it is as characteristic of the events of his body as of his soul. It is impossible to foresee exactly how a man will act; it is equally impossible to foresee, even in a given illness, how he will recover or die. We may obtain a statistic of the average mortality of the disease, as we may obtain another of the average line of conduct of men in certain circumstances; but the individual case can never be perfectly covered.

---

* See analysis on p. 68.

The simple, yet profound reason for this, is, that the spontaneous activities of individuals—mental or physical or both—are themselves the data, and the only data upon which we can construct laws. When we formulate a general law of action, we are simply classing together the circumstances in which the actions or activities of different individual existences agree. But we thereby imply that there must be many more in which they differ, and that each must differ in some respect from all the rest, otherwise there would not be many individuals, but only one.

Thus, in the evident philosophical sense, the assertion, which seems so desolating to Mr. Mallock, that a man was "as automatic as a tree," would be true, because the tree is no more automatic than he. That is to say, the tree being also an individual, the activities of which it is capable, also defy precise calculation. We can only tell approximately that a tree of such a species will be about such a height and shape and color, and bear about such kind of fruit. So long as our knowledge extends no further, we have no knowledge of an individual tree, or real existence, but only of an abstract nominal existence—a class, a genus, a species. When the individual exists, it is a proof that definite currents of life have been started in a definite direction, whose course we can only divine from the characters it will have in common with individual currents already known; which therefore we cannot foresee completely.

The rise in individuality from inorganic to organic nature, from the vegetable to the animal, and from beast to man, is marked by a constant increase in the manifestation of spontaneous activities, consequently in individualization. This progress is continued through successive ranks of human beings. Of the lowest, we can predict their actions with tolerable approach to certainty; but the more highly developed the spiritual nature of a man, the greater the difficulty of foreseeing his thoughts, feelings, or conduct under given circumstances.

Conversely, degradation of human character is marked by successive loss of such power of individualization. The person of weak character conforms passively to the social conditions in which he finds himself; imitates as near as may be the tastes and habits of his associates, until as a technical "imbecile," he reflects "automatically" the actions he sees, without conferring upon them any individual imprint. The insane person becomes completely dominated by some one idea or motion, which effaces the individual peculiarities his personality had previously presented.* The drunkard, in whom, previously to his fit of intoxication, ideas of prudence or compassion may have held in check suggestions of revenge, becomes, when drink has obliterated a part of his personal consciousness, the

* The ideas of the insane, often popularly supposed to be illimited in fantasy, really revolve in an extremely narrow circle; the same delusion reappearing in thousands of cases.

unresisting prey of a single passion, and kills while under its influence.*

Common opinion and common law, recognize therefore a difference in the actions committed by drunkards and by the insane; although also recognizing that the mental condition of such persons is connected by a continuous series of insensible gradations with that of the passionate, the weak, the ignorant, who are held technically responsible. For these latter possess their full personality, such as it is; the others are deprived of a part; they are human beings in the condition of frogs of the Goltz experiment. But what is very noteworthy for the present discussion, the part of which they are deprived is not the will, but a number of the motives which habitually act upon the will, and as a counterpoise to the others now remaining.

From the foregoing consideration it appears that moral responsibility is in no wise diminished by Positive analysis of the phenomena of voluntary action, for any one who is really concerned about the consequences of actions or feelings. It is to these consequences that the Positive method directs attention. It says: "It makes very little difference whether that ugly temper of yours comes from your digestion, or from your insane ancestor, or from evil suspicions from your own mind: it is in any case an equally bad thing, immoral, because constantly disturbing

* We are again much indebted to Griesinger's admirable analysis of the "cessation of the normal internal conflict of ideas," as an essential condition of insanity.

your relations with your fellow beings and injuring them; and it is inherently liable to occasion some greater injury, to which, as a matter of expediency, the civil law limits its punishment. Your responsibility, however, is not limited to a voluntary act which your temper may lead you to commit; it begins already with the inward state of your mind, and demands that you summon to your mind trains of thought and feeling antagonistic to those which have hitherto nourished your evil state of consciousness." *

The "you" that is called upon to make this effort is a mystery because an individual. The effort itself, of which all thinking people have had at least a few occasions to be conscious, is difficult to describe. For our purpose, which is far below the ambition of scientific psychological analysis, and does not rise beyond the desire to prick some of Mr. Mallock's facile fallacies, it is sufficient to notice that this effort is *not* an effort of volition, but simply an effort of attention. Secondly, that the threat of punishment enters as a motive seconding the effort. Finally it is comparatively rare, even for the best disciplined persons, that such distinct efforts are made during the development of moral character. Character is formed by insensible influences, and in almost imperceptible movements, which are incomparably more often involuntary than voluntary. The choice of a man

* It has been noticed that in the great majority of cases insanity begins, not by senseless speeches nor by extravagant acts, but by anomalies of feeling and by the emotional conditions which result from them. Thus the progress to insanity and to vice is made along analogous routes.

who wishes to improve himself in any direction, is to place himself deliberately in a position where he will be exposed to certain influences, or be induced to repeat certain acts rather than others. Mr. Mallock says: "It is clear that if a morality is incapable of being preached, it is useless to say that it is worthy of being practised." (p. 42.) But the Positivist is well aware, on the testimony both of observation and of psychological analysis, that the "preaching of morality" is an agency of uncertain operation and varying strength; an agency moreover that can only influence what is already partly converted. He is inclined to rely upon educational training of the entire nature of a man for the guidance of his moral conduct, so much the more, as he becomes better acquainted with the obscure, unconscious, organic basis, which underlies his distinct consciousness, and whence impulses rise into thoughts, like dim forms rising through deep waters to the surface.

The Positivist preaches no "revival;" but he projects schemes on a vast scale for the development of the moral nature of man; schemes embracing entire generations—involving social institutions—touching upon everything that touches on him, from the clod of earth in which grows the rye or wheat of his bread, to the speculative belief that encloses his life and shapes his actions.

When after this brief analysis, we return to Mr. Mallock's dictum: The Freedom of the will is unintelligible, but as moral beings we must believe in it. We reply:

"There is a sense in which the Freedom of the Will is so unintelligible as to be gibberish, and therefore not to be mentioned in a serious discussion. There is another sense, in which it means the responsibility of conscious beings for their own actions, in which it is not unintelligible at all. The spontaneous action of any individual involves a mystery, that is a hitherto inexplicable, an ultimate fact. But this mystery is the fact of the individuality, and not that of the unimpeded or free action of the individual."

We have not, however, finished with the discussion of will and of free will, for Mr. Mallock continues to consider both under several other aspects than that of "moral necessity." One of these is presented in the form of an ingenious theory, which, as already noticed, the English essayist has borrowed (without acknowledgement) from our American theologian, Bushnell. This is the theory for establishing the supernatural on a basis of fact, by the easy assertion that certain portions of the natural really belong to it. Thus, says Mr. Mallock, as we have already quoted: * "Every action of the human will is a miracle in the strictest sense of the word; only it takes place privately, within the close walls of the brain. The molecules of the brain are arranged and ordered by a supernatural agency. Their natural automatic movements are suspended, or directed and interfered with. * * * God's will is conceived of as dis-

* See p. 132.

turbing the automatic movements of matter without the skull, in just the same way as man's will is conceived of as disturbing those of the brain within it. * * * The erection of a pyramid at the will of an Egyptian king would as much disturb the course of nature as the removal of a mountain by the faith of a Galilean fisherman." (p. 243.)

This is one of the numerous passages in Mr. Mallock's essay which leaves us in doubt whether the author be really as ignorant as he appears, or whether he only presumes on so much ignorance in his readers as may save him the trouble of real thought or acquaintance with what has been often thought, or is perfectly well known.

Mr. Mallock's references to the brain are invariably bewildering. Whether he talks of the brain in a metaphor, or describes what he supposes to be a fact, he betrays a depth of unacquaintance with his subject that is equally dangerous to rhetoric and to argument.

Let us inquire in what the "natural automatic movements of the molecules of the brain" are supposed to result, when they are *not* interfered with by a supernatural agency, or whether this same supernatural agency may be expected to "suspend or direct or interfere with" the movements of the molecules of blood which nourish the brain, or of the arterial walls, or of the heart which throw this blood to the brain, and without which no act of the human will, and therefore no miracle, can possibly take place. When a man becomes unconscious in a fainting fit, where is the supernatural agency? Is it driven out or temporarily annihilated, or has it been so busy with the molecules of the brain that it has forgotten the heart; or does its jurisdiction extend no further than the "closed walls" of its dwelling-place, so that it is liable to be overwhelmed from without by unforeseen combinations?

The whole statement that we have quoted from Mr. Mallock on this matter is so excessively silly that it would seem at first sight hardly worth while to contradict. But to those upon whom by chance it should make the impression of something profound, we would note, that the act of volition, which is supposed to constitute the supernatural agency above mentioned, is itself the result of the very molecular movements of the brain, which are supposed to be suspended. In the absence of volition *no movements take place*—a certain part of the brain remains quiescent. In saying that the volition "results" from these molecular movements, we mean, simply, that the mental and physical conditions are constantly coexistent—the "concave and convex sides of a curve." * If *the molecular movements do not occur, no act of volition is framed; and conversely, if there is no act of volition, there are no molecular movements proceeding "automatically."* What every tyro in physiology knows, but of what Mr. Mallock appears to be naïvely ignorant, is, that the molecular movements which accompany volition and conscious thought are limited to a certain part of the brain—the

* Lewes.—*Physical Basis of Mind.*

cerebral hemispheres—while the "automatic" movements take place in another part, in a series of ganglia situated below those correlated to the sphere of consciousness. This separation between the voluntary and involuntary or "automatic" portions of the brain, is a fact established in the most varied manner by the phenomena of disease and by the results of experiments, analogous to those to which we have already had occasion to refer.

Mr. Mallock quotes a remark from Dr. Tyndall, which, as he does not give us the precise reference, we are unable to compare with the context, and cannot therefore really know the sense in which the great physicist makes it. But our author manipulates the remark in such a fashion as to make it signify that Dr. Tyndall is questioning whether a "state of consciousness can be interposed between the molecules of the brain, and influence the transference of motion among the molecules." (p. 228.) This is exactly as if one should inquire whether a beam of light could be interposed between a couple of the undulations of which itself is composed, and influence the passage of one of those undulations into another. To such an inquiry no answer could possibly be given, and, for obvious reasons we are much more inclined to attribute the question to Mr. Mallock than to Dr. Tyndall. To another quotation from the latter, however, the answer is plain: "Do states of consciousness enter as links into the chain of antecedence and sequence which gives rise to bodily actions ?" (p. 228.) From the facts of the case we are able to answer unhesitatingly, "*Sometimes they do, and sometimes they do not.*" When, impelled by a sensation of hunger, a man bites on a piece of meat, his conscious resolve to do so *is* a link in the chain of sequences between the fact of an empty stomach and the bodily action of taking food. But when the same man during a tetanic spasm, clenches his jaws on a piece of meat, which may, without his resolve, have been placed between them, his consciousness, though acutely sensible of the fact, has nothing to do with its causation. The whole series of sequences lies in the reflex sphere : is accomplished by molecular movements in a series of nervo-muscular organs lying apart from the nerve centres whose activity is essential to consciousness and volition. This upper sphere is disturbed in a certain manner by the nervous actions accomplished below, so that conscious sensibility is awakened. But this is incidental to the series of events itself, external to it, instead of lying within it : and the muscular movement which in health is initiated by a conscious volition, is now caused by a motor impulse with which volition has nothing to do. It is therefore automatic ; the will cannot control it, and, if we may judge from the melancholy history of cases of tetanus, no "supernatural agency," has yet been found able or willing to interfere.

Why the extension of molecular vibrations to a particular part of the brain is accompanied by a manifestation of consciousness, which will remain completely suppressed so long as molecular movements are limited to other parts of the nervous system; *why* it is possible on one occasion to awaken the sensibility of consciousness while leaving quiescent the volition, which on other occasions so readily follow it; whether sensibility is excited only in one part of the hemispheres, and volition in another; whether the molecular vibrations attended by these extraordinary phenomena differ from others in form, or merely in locality in some especial disposition of cerebral structure which enables all vibrations to be focussed into some new and special combination; these are questions some of which we may hope to answer more or less completely by further researches. Some of the questions which really are of "Why" instead of "How" are probably unanswerable, for reasons already stated.* But already enough is known to throw into contempt the shallow wit with which Mr. Mallock fills so many pages in his chapter on "The Logic of Scientific Negation." And we repeat, the two essential facts known which bear upon the subject, are: First, That the activity of a certain part of the brain constitutes a double phenomenon, whose two parts are inseparably, although inexplicably associated; the one part being the physical changes which we *infer*, the other the state of consciousness which we directly *perceive*. Second, That the immense mass of bodily actions are capable of originating in two different

* See pp. 67 and 70.

ways: (*a*) In parts of the nervous system or "centres" lying below the cerebral hemispheres. These actions are automatic, and many of them then cannot be in the least degree controlled by the will; none can be more than slightly influenced. (*b*) These same actions may originate in the cerebral hemispheres, and as these cannot enter into activity or function without a development of consciousness, it is absolutely indifferent whether we say, "A state of consciousness, a volition, the mental aspect of certain molecular movements in the brain, originated such a movement," or, "The physical aspect of this state of consciousness, molecular movements in the cerebral hemispheres originated it."

After this, we deem it superfluous to follow Mr. Mallock into his childish simile of billiard balls, by which he further attempts to demonstrate "a bewilderment, not peculiar to Dr. Tyndall, but characteristic of the whole school he belongs to; inherent in our whole modern Positivism, the whole of our exact and enlightened thought." (p. 231.) Before returning to the question of "miracle" as involved in the human will on the external world, we must however notice two further questions of Mr. Mallock's, because he assures us, that for one of them at least we *must* make a choice. "The first question is, Why should consciousness be connected with the brain at all?" This, Mr. Mallock is kind enough to tell us, "cannot be answered at all," and in relation to it, "we must rest in wonder." "The second question is, What is it when connected? Is it simply the product of the brain's movement; or is the brain's movement in any degree produced by it?" (p. 223.) Mr. Mallock proceeds to tell us that we know the noise made by "the working of the brain's machinery as the crash, the roar, or the whisper of its restless colliding molecules." (p. 224.)

If Mr. Mallock really has heard this, and not imagined it during some fit of sea sickness, he has done more than any authentic person we ever heard of. We can only compare him with clever Alice in Grimm's story, who could see the wind run in the street and hear the flies cough. If he were in the slightest degree acquainted with the laborious researches by which the fact of functional activity of certain portions of the brain, and its co-relation with mental states, has been established, he would know that this is as a matter of *inference*, while the state of consciousness itself, which is directly perceived, was necessarily known long before, in fact was the first thing that ever could be known, as Positivists are perfectly well aware. Mr. Mallock's only idea of an investigation seems to be that of a little boy, who in obedience to orders, goes out to buy cherries, and who, failing to find them, is bound to bring in strawberries instead. Thus he tells us, that "our confessed impotence to form any conjecture at all as to the first" (question), *i. e.*, why consciousness should be connected with the prain, "does not in the least *exonerate* us from choosing between conjectures as to the second." (p. 224.) "Our utter inability to account for the (first) fact, has really no bearing at all upon the great dilemma, the dilemma as to the unity or the dualism of existence, and the independence or automatism of the life and will of man." (p. 224)

Now we confess we do not feel ourselves in the least compelled to limit speculation on the dualism of existence, to such crude conjectures as Mr. Mallock may have to offer us. To modify a little a remark made by him a few pages further on, this demand to stand and deliver a choice, sounds as if one should say: "It is indeed impossible for you to decide whether green cheese is eaten for supper by the inhabitants of the dog star Sirius: but this confessed inability does not in the least exonerate you from the necessity of choosing between two opposite conjectures concerning the shape of the night caps worn by the inhabitants of the star Alpha Hercules." "Are you a Big-endian or a Little-endian?" asked the fiery Lilliputians of Gulliver. We respectfully but firmly reply, "Neither the one nor the other."

Without any "admissions" or "concessions" of incomprehensibles, we may, out of the mouth of Mr. Mallock himself, show a very simple reason why it is impossible to answer the question, "What *is* consciousness?" For to say what a thing *is*, is to assign it a place in a class of similar things. Now as Mr. Mallock himself tells us, "The phenomenon of consciousness is in one way unique." (p. 221.) We should be more bold, we should drop the modifying clauses and declare that, consciousness being an *entirely* unique phenomenon, can be compared with nothing else. It cannot be classified, for there is nothing else to be put into the same class with it. When we say, "what is a rose?" the answer can be given, "a rose is a flower." But when we are asked, "what is consciousness?" We can only reply, "consciousness is consciousness." Or, the nearest approach to classification which can be made, "consciousness is an ultimate fact, the first with which we are acquainted, the fact of which we are more sure than of anything else, even than of the testimony of our senses." We would remind Mr. Mallock if it be necessary, that it was not a Positivist who said, "I think, therefore I am." But Positivism would reject as superfluous the implication of an inference contained in the "therefore;" would content itself with saying, "I am." And it is a principle of Positivism, in emphatic contradictions here as elsewhere with the principles of Catholicism, that the existence of one ultimate fact can never be invalidated by knowledge of the existence of another, whatever obscurity may rest on the relations between them.

Hence we are at a loss to imagine whence Mr. Mallock finds the grounds for his assertion that physical science "is supposed to have triumphantly unified the apparent dualism of things," (p. 220). It is true that Mr. Mallock cannot mention this subject without involving himself in palpable contradictions; for, in the very sentence just quoted, where he tells us that physical science has unified dualism, he says that this is because it has "completely *connected* mind with matter." Now two things which are connected, *remain* two; only upon further information must we suppose that they have been made into one.

Again, this same physical science "has revealed consciousness to us as a function of the brain, and as altogether inseparable from it." It is true we cannot think of a function apart from the organ exercising it; but still less (if possible,) can we think of a function as being the *same thing* as that organ. As well assert that a symphony was identical with the violins of the orchestra which played it, or that all the ideas and emotions awakened by the music were simply pieces of the resin with which the performers rubbed their bows.

Precisely this ridiculous assertion is what Mr. Mallock does attribute constantly and gratuitously to the Positivists. He does so for two reasons, which, though real enough in themselves, are very different from the philosophical and moral ones he pretends them to be. In the first place he wishes to prove, not only that consciousness is something different from the brain, but that the soul is an entity capable of surviving the body; and he will not forgive the Positivists for insisting that this is not a philosophical question at all, but, if anything, a question of fact, to be decided by future experience. And in the second place, it is perfectly impossible for Mr. Mallock, in his utter destitution of biological training, to conceive of a function, to think of it as an immaterial relation, or to think of combined relations as resulting in something radically and necessarily different from the elements which enter into them. He cannot believe that any thing can ever grow or develop into something which it had not always been. Although the commonest experience of every day life shows him absolutely unconscious and passive new born babies, developing into beings so different as to seem scarcely to belong to the same order of things; when a slight extension of this common observation, would show that the development had proceeded from an even lower plane than appeared at birth; that it proceeded from a more senseless mass,—from an almost inperceptible cell;—in spite of this simple, indisputable observation, Mr. Mallock, and others like him, persist in asserting that whatever establishes relations between mental and physical conditions, asserts their identity; and whoever shows how to a world of matter has become superadded a world of mind, has tried to demonstrate that no world of mind ever existed. "Matter existed and fermented* long before the evolution of mind; mind is not an exhibition of new forces, but the outcome of a special combination of the old." (p. 220). So far as observation can teach us, the chronology of this statement is correct; but the doctrine of evolution does not deny the *newness* of the forces which are the outcome of the old, any more than it denies the *newness* of the young which are the offspring of parents.

* Does Mr. Mallock think that the matter in the body of a developing fœtus is "fermenting?"

Where is the new to come from if not from the old?

In respect to consciousness, however, "physical observations" are not, as Mr. Mallock supposes, "the only things to guide us." Physical observations, indeed, acquire for us an immense amount of valuable information about the relations of consciousness with the physical condition of the body of the conscious individual, and even with the medium in which that body is placed. But the phenomena of consciousness themselves, their mutual relations and their laws, are the subject of *psychical* observation. To suppose that the finest physiological analysis would ever suffice for the study of mental laws, would be like supposing that chemical analysis would suffice to explain the laws of the position of bodies in space.* As already said, this physical and mental side of consciousness once developed must be studied along two indefinitely converging lines, whose point of convergence is known positively to exist, is felt, but cannot be seen. But no Positivist thinker would dream of coalescing these two lines, nor of asserting that "sorrow" was a molecule, because a profound melancholy may be engendered by a disordered digestion. Nor that "thoughts" and "affections have a certain bulk in space," because they may not only be studied psychically, but be made the subject of "physical experiment,"† when a dose of opium quickens the imagination, or a dose of alcohol has pro-

* We do not deny that some rash persons *have* supposed this, but it is far from being a principle of Positivism.

† See p. 212 of Mallock's Essay.

duced a state of maudlin sentiment. And the "suppressed premise, that nothing exists but what the study of matter conceivably could reveal to us: or that, in other words, the immaterial equals the non-existent," (p. 214) is a premise which exists nowhere except in the fancy of such speculators as Mr. Mallock. No study of matter could reveal our consciousness to us if that were not already known long before we began any serious and deliberate study of matter. And even in the study of matter, the immaterial relations of things, as they are conceived by the mind, are studied with at least as much interest and belief as are its sensible properties.

So much for "supernatural" disturbance of the automatic molecules of the brain by which "miracles" are supposed to be wrought "privately within its closed walls." Let us now consider the external miracle, alleged almost in the same breath—the disturbance of the uniform course of nature by human volition.

It is one of many illustrations of the impossibility experienced by theological thought of keeping entirely clear from the influences of modern times, that the idea of a uniform course of nature has become so important and necessary that any one may now venture to call any disturbance of uniformities a miracle.

It is well known that the original conception of miracles was very different from this: it suggested no extraordinary interference with a "uniform course of nature," because nobody was at all sure that the course of nature was uniform. A miracle was simply a wonder, and a wonder without any real point of comparison with events held to be non-miraculous. The course of nature is only uniform so long as all the conditions remain the same. Any line of invariable sequence may be changed by starting another line which crosses it at any point. This new line may be under the operation of precisely the same law as the old: as when a barrel which was rolled down hill by the force of gravitation, remains in stable equilibrium through the operation of the same force; or it may involve a simpler law, as when a bullet passed through a man's heart, withdraws his body from the domain of laws of living organisms, and places it under the operation of laws of the chemical affinities of organized but dead matter. Or finally, it may bring into play a more complex law, as when the chemical affinities of an acid suffice to overcome the molecular cohesion of a stone; or when the vital action of the heart distributes blood in a vertical direction, notwithstanding the influence of gravity; or when molecular movements in the volitional centres of the brain result in a discharge of nerve force, by means of which the habitual tonus of a muscle is overcome, and thereby a limb displaced.

What does the Egyptian king do when he builds a pyramid, and raises a structure towards the sky in "defiance" of the law of gravity which should make it fall to the earth? Mr. Mallock cannot be so ignorant as not to know that he accomplishes this feat by obedience to this same law of gravity; and if that were really suspended, his pyramid might as easily float off into the air. We are almost ashamed to repeat what has been pointed out so often, namely, that the operation of man's will in disturbing the uniformities of nature, is only possible so long as he can rely on analogous or identical uniformities. That the "fixed course of nature" does not mean that all natural circumstances must always remain as they are; but that any series of events tends to repeat itself in the same manner until interrupted by some other series. That combinations of circumstances governed by simple laws, are stable in proportion to their simplicity; and that conversely, every increase in the complexity of the combination renders the equilibrium more unstable, and the circumstances more easily modifiable. Thus, as Comte has observed, the combinations of circumstances which we can most readily predict, are those over which we have the least influence; while others, whose extreme complexity defies calculation, are precisely those which can be changed most readily by the human will, effecting new combinations. Examples of the first are the cosmic conditions of the universe; of the second, physiological, psychological and social events, the proper sphere for the free action of the human will.*

The Positivist conception of the power of human thought and will to change the condition of the world

---

* Physical and chemical phenomena occupy an intermediate position in both these respects.

rises far above that of a capricious thaumaturgy. It is understood that whenever the elements of a situation have become thoroughly known, they may be combined into a different situation, into something entirely new. Thus a double incentive is offered to analysis; intensely interesting in itself, it is of immeasurable value as the only possible road to synthesis. Knowledge is the stepping stone to creation, and science finds its complement and ultimate horizon in art. From the fact above mentioned, that it is the most complex conditions which are the most liable to modification, it follows that the conditions of life, individual and social, which are the most interesting to human beings, are precisely those which are the most amenable to his control. Yet, not only theory but experience shows that his power of control extends beyond and below this human sphere—extends into the physical world, into which human agency enters as a permanently modifying force, together with the winds and the waves, with the currents of air and of sea, with storms and sunshine, and with blind, far-reaching instincts in tree and flower, in insect, bird and beast. It is not undignified companionship, and it is one recognized but recently. The moment of such recognition is also the moment for recognizing the immense supremacy of the human force, conscious and guided by knowledge, over that of the blind, unconscious forces by which it is surrounded, and in the midst of which it works.

The consideration of free will as a "miraculous" agency

might be called, in Mr. Mallock's terminology, the "intellectual aspect" of the case. We are aware, however, that for him the "moral necessities" are the most important. Besides the "individual necessity" we have already discussed, there is another of wider range which we must now consider.

Mr. Mallock affirms, as the result of various observations, that "a certain supernatural moral judgment has become a primary faculty with us, and mixes with every estimate we form of the world around us." (p. 133.)

We will not stop to ask how any faculty can *become* primary if it is not so from the beginning. It is more important to consider the succeeding assertion: "It is this faculty which Positivism, if accepted fully, must destroy or paralyze." The following is the argument: "Happiness naturally would seem the test of right, [but] right has come supernaturally to be the test of happiness.* * * In all our deeper views of life, whether we be saints or sinners, right and wrong are the things that first appeal to us, not happiness or misery." (p. 133.) That is, this is what happens until the blighting influence of Positivism comes in the way. Then all sense of moral distinctness is destroyed, and the only test of the correctness of any line of conduct is the amount of happiness, *i.e.* pleasure, it may obtain. Thus this "supernatural" moral judgment is eliminated from life, or rather would be if Positivism were allowed to succeed.*

* Still the same semi-military idea, that Positive thought is not a speculation to be investigated, but an enemy to be put down.

In order to obtain some idea of the state of life after such elimination, Mr. Mallock passes in review certain great works of art in order to show that the interest in them centres about some moral conflict, which becomes meaningless so soon as we imagine for a moment that the "impassioned struggle for a supernatural right is suspended." Thus our author shows, as it is easy to show, that the real tragedy of "Macbeth" "does not lie in the fact that Duncan is murdered, but in the fact that Macbeth is the murderer. * * * What our minds are made to dwell upon is not that Duncan shall sleep forever, but that Macbeth shall sleep no more." "In 'Hamlet' the action that an interest centres in, is the hero's struggle to conform to an internal personal standard of right, utterly irrespective of use to others, or of natural happiness to himself." "In the 'Antigone' we have for the central interest the same personal struggle after right, not after use or happiness." "In 'Measure for Measure' and 'Faust' we can see at once that one moral judgment, at least, is, before all things, presupposed in us. This is a hard and fixed judgment with regard to female chastity and the supernatural value of it."

Two reasons are alleged to show that Positivism must destroy interest in these dramas and in the life corresponding to them. 1st. That the Positive conception of morality is not moral at all, but refers to something that is contradicted by these dramas and by all life which is on as high a plane as they; and, 2d, that "the grand relation of man is not first to his brother men, but to something else that is beyond humanity—that is at once without and also beyond himself; to this first, and to his brother men through this. We are not our own; we are bought with a price. Our bodies are God's temples, and the joy and the terror of life depends on our keeping these temples pure or defiling them." (p. 139.)

To speak of this second assertion first, we may observe that it would be scarcely possible to choose more unfortunate examples for the thesis. In every one of the dramas selected, the motive involves a most profound moral relation to a fellow creature. Now it is a treacherous violation of confidence, as when Macbeth murders his royal guest, or Faust seduces and abandons his innocent and helpless lover. Now it is an heroic and steadfast loyalty, as when Antigone, at the peril of her life, performs the funeral rites of her brother. Now it is the cowardly failure to perform an act of vengeance, justly demanded by filial piety, as when Hamlet, in the very fruition of his project, recoils from the exposure of the king. In "Measure for Measure" alone the heroism is not aroused for the sake of another, but in self-defense against an act of intolerable baseness on the part of a person above all to be trusted—a brother. We are told at the outset that these tragedies appeal to a "moral judgment *in us*." Why is the ground so suddenly shifted to something "without and beyond us?" By what looseness of rhetoric can the Pauline metaphor of being "bought with a price" be made to apply here? *Who* is bought? and why? and for what price?

Considering the theological beliefs which prevailed at the time that each of the five selected dramas were written, it is remarkable how little *religion* in any other sense than that of imperative and binding* duty, intervenes in them. Antigone, indeed, has no language in which to express a sense of duty, except as obedience to a direct fiat of the gods. The importance attached to the rite of sepulchre was not however a moral but a religious importance, and, as appertaining to a now decayed religion, we presume that even Mr. Mallock would be more inclined to call it superstitious than supernatural. But it is not this superstition, but the fraternal loyalty and the heroism that responded to its mandates, which have immortalised Antigone for us. It is not the so-called divine element which has made the human element interesting: it is the human element, the human emotion and courage which have preserved from oblivion the ordinance once celebrated as divine.

In the Shakespearean plays, the pure *humanity* of the interest is still more obvious. Macbeth is absorbed by his crime, and no foreboding of hell is added to the weight of his conscious guilt. Hamlet reasons about a future life with all the skepticism, if not with all the calm

* Well known to be the original meaning of the term "religion."

of the author of Ecclesiastes, and neither in his condemnation of the criminals, nor in his own self-upbraidings, does he require to pass beyond contemplation of the deed itself to feel to the core its awful significance. The only "supernatural" circumstance in the play is the ghost; and the greatness and truth of Shakespeare's art is shown not least in this, that the ghost is allowed to make so little impression upon us, and so little real difference to Hamlet. He had known its message in advance, and the spectral vision was but the outward projection of his own inmost conviction. He who could not listen to this, would not be, and was not spurred to action, though one rose from the dead.

The same perversity which makes Mr. Mallock to misinterpret these great dramas, leads him to identify the motive of "Measure for Measure" with that of "Faust." We are thus told that the seduction of Margaret by her real love, was identical with the proposed sale of Isabella to a brutal ravisher: that the crime in the one case did not lie in the desertion by Faust, nor in the other in the betrayal by a brother, but in both consisted entirely in the fact that the heroines were unmarried women. We should infer that, in Mr. Mallock's view, if Faust had married Margaret before running away, or if Isabella had been persuaded into marriage with the Duke in order to save her cowardly brother, that the "supernatural" and artistic interest of both stories would be destroyed.

It is of course a well known Catholic idea that "a supernatural value attaches to female chastity," but what sense Mr. Mallock attaches to this phrase we own we fail to discover. It can scarcely mean a value derived from another world, for if ever virtue were inseparably associated with the earthly and fleshly conditions of this life, it is evidently the virtue of chastity. If used in the sphere of being a virtue maintained in spite of "natural" instincts, and in obedience to a new classification of values whereby "many things naturally repellant have received a supernatural blessing, and many things naturally pleasant have received a supernatural curse," (p. 133) we might understand how Margaret should be accused of violating it; but the virtue of Isabella remains still unexplained. In no supposition could we imagine that *she* was tempted to anything "naturally pleasant;" she was, on the contrary, threatened with something horribly repellent.

We suppose that Mr. Mallock really means that if our moral judgment had not been trained to attach an incalculable value to the absolute innocence of girls, that there would have been no social infamy to ruin Margaret and madden her to infanticide; hence the conduct of Faust himself would have been blameless, or at least as indifferent as that of one who picks a flower in his path, and, having inhaled its perfume, throws it aside. And that, with a similar state of public opinion, the proposition made by Isabella's brother would have been a mere appeal to her ordinary good nature, which all affectionate sisters might justly condemn her for refusing.

It is perfectly true that in the absence of a profound social ideal in regard to this central relation of human beings with each other, art could imagine no tragedies dependent upon it. Conceivable also that powerful and strenuous interests would disappear from our complex life by the levelling of certain difficulties exclusively created by the "faculty of moral judgment." But it is equally true, as Mr. Mallock himself has said, that this moral judgment is *in us*, and not the echo of a voice from heaven or the vision of the descent of any Holy Ghost upon earth. It is a most complex moral judgment, whose constitution can be analzed to many elements, and whose history can be traced to many origins. It is a fact as perfectly well known as is the evolution of mind from the body of every human babe, that the social judgment upon the relations of the sexes varies with every radical variation in the general status of society. Ideals on this subject are among the most elaborate and refined products of social consciousness. Even more than others are they necessarily correlated to the essential conditions of social existence at any given time, for the simple reason that they determine the extent and nature of the family, the unit of the social organism.

The ideal is evidently different in the tribes who captured their wives from without, and thought it disgraceful to marry their tribal kin; in those who reverse the disgrace, and invoke it upon foreign marriages; in polygamic civilizations; among peoples governed by Athenian horror of barbarians, or by Roman law; among those in whom a logical asceticism creates an ideal of absolute celibacy, from which marriage is a degradation only palliated as a matter of necessary compromise by the sacraments of the Church; or, finally,* among those who, seeing in love, and in the fact of the origin of life in love, the central fact of life, study love and marriage and parentage in their real relations with the facts of life, and associate with ideas of chastity, and purity, and honor in love reverence so much the more profound, as these are seen to have been evolved in the course of a social development perfectly natural. From this point of view indeed, it would be difficult to enforce virtue by the savage reflection,

"She died, she went to burning flame." †

But as this reflection has proved tolerably inoperative, even when its justice was undisputed, it is little likely that much coercive force can be obtained from its revival. Unless indeed we believe, as Mr. Mallock may, that the ghost of a belief, as of a person, exercises a more powerful

---

* We say finally as a matter of expediency, not to extend too far allusions to the innumerable variations in the laws of marriage, and consequently in the "hard and fixed judgment" to which Mr. Mallock attributes a "supernatural sameness."

† "She died, she went to burning flame,
She mixed her ancient blood in shame.
The wind is howling in turret and tree.
So, morn and evening at his gate
To win his love I lay in wait,
Oh, the Earl was fair to see!"
Tennyson's Sisters.

influence on the imagination than the same in full vigor of life.

How now shall there remain any plausibility in the assertion that the Positivist conception of morality is not moral at all, but in flagrant contradiction with the fundamental conception of these great works of art?

The plausibility depends on the previous assertion, that, to the Positivist, happiness is the only test of right, because that is the *natural* test of right; whereas in the dramas, and in the high plane of life corresponding to them, right is the test of happiness. So soon, says Mr. Mallock, as you deny the possibility of a "supernatural blessing and curse," you are compelled to accept as your highest good, whatever may be desired by the promptings of natural instinct.

Here again we meet with decisive proof of the impossibility of conceiving of the Positive doctrine of morals without thorough acquaintance with the biological doctrine of evolution; proof again of the correctness of Comte's law, exacting study of biology as an indispensable preparation to the study of moral as of any other social relations.

The biological fact which is of importance in this place is common to all organized beings, and completely explains Mr. Mallock's imposing paradox of the "supernatural classification" "traversing" the natural one. The fact is, that in the course of development of an organism a set of conditions is often reached, not merely different from those of our earlier stage, but exactly the reverse of them. Thus, to select only the most common examples, the tail of the tadpole becomes replaced by the legs of the frog; the immobility of the chrysalis for the airy fluttering of the butterfly; the placental respiration of the fœtus for the pulmonary respiration of the new born. Thus the same creature is compelled to change its classification of pleasantnesses, and even of necessities, merely because in the course of its natural evolution the conditions of its existence have changed. Quite similarly, in the course of the evolution of society, the moral law and moral taste have changed, not according to the "caprice of any one man," but according to the changed life of all. The "supernatural" value of the Sabbath day has declined. The "natural" value of honor and loyalty has increased. So much as to entirely preponderate over the "supernatural" impulse to offer by force or treachery one's fellow creatures as a sacrifice to one's own Deity, whether the massacre be commanded at Canaan or on St. Bartholomew's day. While, perhaps, the most remarkable change ever wrought during the evolution of the moral sense, is that by which an ideal of reserved spiritual love has been developed out of the primitive nucleus of promiscuous physical passion.*

* As the question in the text relates especially to the manner in which later conditions may *reverse* earlier ones, without for that reason becoming in the least supernatural, we insert in a note merely the following passage from Comte, which bears too much on the general subject to be entirely omitted : "In its most profound appreciation, Positivism represents human progress as always consisting in a simple development of the fundamental

To return to the original statement. The Positivists, says Mr. Mallock, *talk* indeed about morality, and make a great fuss over it, but when we come to sift their assertions we find that we do not know what they are talking about. It is true, he continues "the Positivist conceives of the moral end in the same way, and sets upon it the same value" [as the Theist] (p. 95). But while the premises of the Theist enable him to give a perfectly "logical and full account of the nature of the moral end and of its supposed importance," the premises of the Positivist must leave its disciples to break down altogether.

According to Mr. Mallock, Theism and Positivism agree in ascribing three primary characteristics to the moral end. It is "inward and inalienable;" it is "of an importance great out of all proportion to our own consciousness of the results of it;" and "its standard is absolute, beyond and above the taste of any single man or of any body of men." *

The way that Theism "logically" demonstrates the reality of these characteristics is as follows: It shows the importance of the moral end in the first place by "con-

---

order, which necessarily contains the germs of all the progress possible. The true theory of our nature, individual or collective, demonstrates that the cause of our transformations can never depend on a creation, and only on an evolution. This general principle is fully confirmed by an appreciation of history, which, for each mutation accomplished, always succeeds in discovering the roots in some anterior epoch; finding even in the grossest primitive conditions the rudimentary sketch of all ulterior perfections."—Loc. cit., p. 106.

* See p. 21.

fessing fully" that it cannot be shown at all "from the facts in life." Now, inasmuch as every moral law we can think of relates to these facts of life, one might suppose that this was a rather serious confession of impotence. But not at all, for here as elsewhere, Mr. Mallock's confessed inability to walk on plain ground, only serves to exhibit more clearly his agility in floating above it in the upper air. Thus, the Theist having confessed himself to be so much less able than the Positivist claims to be, goes on to say that this importance of the moral end "can at present be divined and augured only; its value is one of promise rather than of performance; and the possession itself is a thing that passes understanding. It belongs to a region of mystery into which neither logic nor experiment will ever suffice to carry us; and whose secrets are beyond the reach of any intellectual aëronaut." (p. 93.)

Upon reading the above sentence, a remark rose to our lips, which however we found, on turning the page, that Mr. Mallock had literally taken out of our mouth. "Nothing would be gained, however, by postulating merely a mystery—an unknowable." We seem, therefore, to be no better off than we were before. But Theism, having "postulated" in the freest manner possible, the first mystery, naturally experienced no difficulty in going further, and postulating anything which may be necessary to make this available. A connection is established between man and the mystery by means of the "two distinctive doctrines, the existence of a personal God, and his own personal immortality." The effect of the first doctrine or "theory" as Mr. Mallock calls it, is that the Theist "feels an eye ever upon him," and reading his inward thoughts, which therefore must be conformed to the moral law as well as the outward actions. "The standard of morality is God's will and not man's immediate happiness." "Man's primary duty is toward God, his secondary duty is towards his brother man; and it is only from the filial relation that the fraternal springs." The Theist does not profess to know the real reasons for "his highest moral actions," but nevertheless he enjoys great "peace and gladness in them," because they "reach far away beyond the earth and its destinies, and connect him with some timeless and holy mystery." (pp. 94-95.).

It is very true that the Positivist can do none of these fine things, for he can see no reason for doing so. He cannot even understand what is meant by a "*timeless* mystery," nor why something outside of the earth is necessarily more holy than something on its surface. Were it so, the tail of a comet should excite more moral and religious enthusiasm than the heroism of a man or woman risking their lives on this planet for the sake of strangers in a pestilence. The Positivist, remembering that the admitted uselessness of the first mystery is only said to have been dissipated by the introduction of new doctrines, feels that still more are required to explain the mysteries which are left. "Nothing is gained" by asserting that the standard of morals is God's will, until we are supplied with some means of knowing what that will is.

A superficial glance at history shows that the ten commandments are by no means the only summary of morals which has been offered to mankind with the stamp of divine sanction. Not the least ingenious systems are those which have claimed to find in every impulse of nature, a revelation of the will of the creator of nature; systems which, whether practically realized among Gnostics or Anabaptists, or theoretically conceived by Fourier, have lead to conclusions the reverse of convenient.

The three "characteristics" of the moral law described by Mr. Mallock are not its only attributes, nor, perhaps, the most important, and from among them Positivism decidedly rejects one, *i. e.*, absoluteness. This character indeed *cannot* be deduced from even the Theistic postulate, that the standard is God's will. For unless society always staid the same, the supposed means of obeying this will must be different at different times. They differ when (according to Mr. Mallock) Antigone tried to obey it by performing a rite of sepulchre, which, in obedience to another very plausible opinion about God's will, had been forbidden. Or when a pious Jew, endeavoring to please God by reminding him of his success in the creation, laid down to sleep in sacred idleness throughout the Sabbath Day. Or when Cotton Mather, wishing to glorify God by defying the works of the devil, burned at the stake the old witch-women who were the most palpable incarnation of the same. But why multiply illustrations? Have we not already learned from Mr. Mallock himself, that Theism without a Catholic Revelation to interpret it, is "a religion of little help; that it never puts out a hand to lift or lead them; [that] it is an alluring voice heard far off through a fog, and calling to them, 'Follow me!' but it leaves them in the fog to pick their own way out towards it, over rocks and streams and pitfalls, which they can but half distinguish, and amongst which they may be either killed or crippled, and are almost certain to grow bewildered." (p. 266.)

When we have once learned that this severe estimate of Theism is awaiting us at one end of Mr. Mallock's essay, we cannot but doubt whether such vague comfort be really capable of offering as "strictly logical a basis" for mortals as is asserted at the beginning.

To assert that the moral law is absolute in a philosophical sense, *i. e.*, as having no relations with anything, would be manifestly absurd, because even on Mr. Mallock's hypothesis that it consists of a fiat of Deity, it embraces relations between the man commanded and the act he is to perform, and that act involves other persons or things in mutual relations.

We suppose, however, that Mr. Mallock means merely that, when a commandment has been given, as "Thou shalt not kill," it holds good in all times, for all places, and for all people. Indeed, the antithesis to absolute established by our author, is precisely, variation according to individual taste. Yet this definition will not hold, even of such a command as that forbidding murder, for it is lawfully evaded whenever the killing is to be effected on a large scale in war; or when the sacrifice of life, though less direct, is scarcely less certain, as when a railroad is to be built through a pestilential country, However, although "absoluteness" cannot be predicated by the moral law, the independence of individual caprice, which Mr. Mallock so oddly imagines to be an equivalent to it, certainly can be. It can be in the same manner, and for the same reason, as the independence of any law must be similarly asserted. It must not be forgotten that there are two entirely distinct meanings to the term "law." The first is indeed a "code of restraining orders," promulgated by some legislative authority, and accompanied by a train of arbitrary penalties, whose infliction is intrusted to a powerful executive. It is well known that the original idea of moral law was exactly that of such a code, whose promulgation and enforcement were modelled upon the examples of human states, but whose originator and avenger were supposed to be divine. Well known also that the moral laws announced as emanating from divine sources were of the most heterogeneous description, involving quite as many precepts of pure ritual that have since become obsolete, as of commands of such permanent utility that they may still be retained. This is true even of the Ten Commandments, which we suppose Mr. Mallock would consider a perfect type of an "absolute" moral law. The law for the observance of the Sabbath day is placed on precisely the same plane as the laws against murder, theft and adultery. It is almost superfluous to notice further that in other Theisms than the Jewish, obedience to the declared will of one God was often sufficient to draw down upon the pious the wrath of another. Mr. Mallock himself points out to us that the Christian Deity, from an external point of view, may be said to have acquired his sovereignty as did the Roman Cæsar. He absorbed into his own person the offices of all the gods that were before him, as the Roman Cæsar absorbed all the offices of the state (p. 20), and thus the executive authority which punished became identified with the legislature which announced its "absolute" decrees.

The second and modern conception of the moral law is based on the type, not of criminal jurisprudence, but of the natural laws of physical phenomena. It is only "absolute" therefore in the same sense in which they are; that is, it is the true expression of the real relations of certain things, and cannot therefore be changed by any individual estimate of these relations, based, not on observation, but on caprice and interested motive.

But what are the relations expressed by the moral law? What things are involved in these relations? No things are involved except actions. With this assertion the Positivism of modern thought at once sweeps away an immense mass of material formerly subjected to moral law and religious emotion; sweeps away the sanctities and accursedness, the purity and uncleanness, which formerly attached to innumerable *things*, and must still attach in the opinion of any one who believes in the power of holy water, of sacred inunctions, of blessed formulæ obtaining "grace and mercy through set channels." Only *persons* can be involved in the moral laws, and the Positivist conception differs from the theological in this: that while for the latter the persons are the [divine] lawgiver and the mortal who is to obey him; for the former, the persons are both human beings, who have learned by experience that they must act in a certain way, under penalty of being unable to act together at all. *The moral law therefore, is the law of the most fundamental conditions of the concerted actions of two or more human beings.* It is not the only law, but it is the most fundamental, since its violation tends more than any other to annihilate the possibility of some class of actions. Thus, all social relations imply mutual confidence in the truth, honesty and friendliness of the persons engaging in them; confidence which varies in depth and extent according to the importance of the interests at stake. Were universal falsehood and treachery substituted, every man would avoid his fellows like wild beasts; as indeed he often has done for this reason. On the other hand, in proportion as honesty refines into honor, and justice into sympathy, the bands of association are drawn closer, social relations become not only possible, but delightful; social existence is not only created, but embellished, and enters upon a development whose expansion scarcely knows a limit. The importance, therefore, which the Positivist, no less than Mr. Mallock, attributes to the moral law, is derived from its inseparable connection with the conditions of existence of the actions to which it refers. It is of primary importance in comparison with all other laws, because referring to primary conditions, while those only relate to secondary ones. Thus the economic laws governing commercial relations, important though they be, can never take the place of the primary law necessitating a general average of fair dealing. A preponderance of fraudulent transactions must sooner or later bring the business to a stand-still. The importance of moral laws is not equal, but according to the degree to which the conditions it imposes are fundamental. Thus, however important sympathy, justice is even more important; and no benevolence nor tenderness of feeling can make up for the absence of truth. This natural gradation in the value of moral laws, is the first reason for denying to them the attribute of absoluteness. Their importance is relative to the importance of the respective actions in maintaining or in developing social relations.

This is the first relativity; but there is a second. The moral life of human beings is partly a spontaneous existence and partly a self-creation. The capacity for creating ideals, upon which we have already insisted, involves a constant liability to change in the definition of the same relations. What is just, at a time that different classes of people have become habituated to radically different kinds of treatment, may be horribly unjust when equality of rights and consequently of expectations has been established. Entire equality of rights implies entire equality of natures; and as the latter equality does not really exist, the former will never exist in the moral law; the equality in civil law representing only a gross approximation to it. We have already dwelt upon the curious manœuvre by which the Catholic church created an artificial and absolute equality in salvation, by means of a universal system, half dogma, half ritual, which being external to the varying nature of human capacities, could be applied indiscriminately to all.* Such an equality is certainly rejected by Positivism.

The influence of created ideals is felt perhaps especially in regard to a class of actions and of moralities, where it is most difficult to apply a test of apparent utility and of immediate happiness for the persons directly involved. This is the class whose morality is love, and whose immorality is vice. It is constantly asserted by Mr. Mallock, with an air of great triumph, that, in the absence of a positive, precise and absolute mandate from heaven, the sentiments and actions belonging to this class, at least, can have no other rule for guidance than personal taste and caprice, and these from the nature of things and from

* See p. 116.

the vicious inclinations of man, are quite as likely to incline to vice as to virtue, to build up a city of "Sodom as the tents of Abraham."

We have already seen, however, that it is especially in regard to this class of actions that society establishes its most strenuously defended ideals; ideals whose precise character varies somewhat at different stages of its evolution, but which always have this in common, that they are the product of the collective social consciousness, are felt to be correlated to the most profound conditions of existence, and cannot be violated without risk of social obloquy. The maintenance of such ideals is secured not only by means of direct appreciation of their value, but by means of the struggle to defend certain rights which they may have conferred, and which could only be abandoned after a universal abandonment of the ideal. Thus, it is conceivable that such a state of public opinion might prevail, that husbands and wives would cease to be shocked at each others' infidelities, would become so entirely indifferent to them that neither would dream of protesting against a violation of *rights* on the part of the other. Adultery then, which to-day is condemned on somewhat the same basis as theft and murder,* would soon cease to be condemned at all; and history shows us many epochs at which this state of things *has* tended more or less completely to prevail. Until it does, however, adul-

* Mr. Mallock asserts the contrary, and thinks Mr. Huxley a fool for saying so.

tery tends to be repressed by all the force which the passion of jealousy and the association of honor can lend to love, whose very existence is menaced by the tolerated crime. Neither civil tribunal nor church anathema can enforce the law; the battle is to be fought, and always has been fought, ever since an ideal of pure and constant love has existed, between those who cleave to it on the one hand, and those who degrade it on the other.

Whenever it occurs that the universal change in a social ideal of any morality, is proved by experience to be attended by good consequences instead of bad; *i.e.* when other moralities are intensified instead of weakened, other energies rendered more powerful, and the bands of society drawn closer instead of relaxing, then such a change establishes its own legitimacy.

How does Mr. Mallock expect this moral law to be enforced otherwise than as we have described? He tells us that when the Positivists have made of the moral law "nothing absolute" they have left it "incapable of being enforced." But how does this absoluteness help the enforcement? and how will Mr. Mallock distinguish what *is* absolute? Even the church, he tell us, has tolerated and even adopted many "pious opinions;" among others that of the celibacy of the clergy. Does Mr. Mallock hold that Luther was therefore guilty when he married his Catharine? or does he think that the right of a father to dispose of his daughter in marriage is as absolute as that of a husband to refuse to dispose of his wife at all?

Mr. Mallock cannot be unaware that, not so long ago, the first right was generally acknowledged, and the last right—at least among the peasants of some countries, generally disputed. Has the church pronounced on these matters?

Has Bellarmine, whose opinion on the situation of purgatory seems to have been so grossly misunderstood by Sir James Stephen (p. 292), left us any authentic testimony on right and wrong, on purity and impurity of love?

Positivism of course can dispense easily with such testimony. It studies love in itself, examines what makes it strong and mighty, what saps its strength, fritters its resources, and reduces it to a frivolous fancy—a dissolute caprice. It searches into the effects upon society of the strong love and the weak one; it sees that the dissolution of love leads ultimately to the dissolution of society—that the strong passion leads to the great life; and it condemns or approves with an energy into which is poured the unconscious forces of existence.

On the other hand, having no artificial end in view, but only the real interests of what it conceives of as real and legitimate, Positivism does not hesitate to sweep away laws which may be shown to conflict with those interests. Thus it has already condemned the absoluteness of parental authority over marriage; thus, perhaps, it may condemn some other customs still maintained. But both in the construction of ideals and in the criticism of ideals,

Positivism judges a sentiment or an action according to the laws of their own nature, and *relatively* to their origin, their effects, and their relations with other things recognized as also of real importance.

Nothing can be more untrue, therefore, than Mr. Mallock's assertion that the Positivists "isolate the moral law from any law or force in the universe that may be wider and more permanent." (p. 96.) On the contrary, the law of moral things is shown to be linked in innumerable ways to the law of physical things which has preceded it in development. It is, indeed, "no longer a thing we can talk vaguely about, or to which any soundings but indefinite phrases will be applicable." (p. 97.) But it is only a person of Mr. Mallock's peculiar perversity of mind who could record this as a reproach.

So much for the Positivist view of the importance and absoluteness of the moral law. In regard to the "inwardness" alleged also to be an essential characteristic, we encounter a singular assertion from our author. "The moral end is an inward state of the heart; and the heart, on the showing of the Positivists, is for each man an absolute solitude." (p. 98.) In proof of this Mr. Mallock quotes several stanzas of poetry from Matthew Arnold and George Eliot, and even from Bishop Keble, who could hardly be accused of having been a Positivist. This association of names itself shows the absurdity of the statement that "the solitude of each man's heart" is a peculiarly Positivist doctrine. It is impossible, moreover, to see in what way this statement can serve as a basis for that which is made to follow it as a deduction. "Such is the condition of the individual according to the Positivist theory. It is evident, therefore, that one of the first results of Positivism is to destroy even the rudiments of every machinery by which one man could govern with authority the inward kingdom of another, and the moral imperative is reduced to an empty vaunt." (p. 99.) But where did such machinery ever exist? Where was one man, even though he were Pope of Rome, ever able to exercise more than a semblance of government over the "inward kingdom" of another? The "moral imperative" has always been an "empty vaunt" so far as it professed to judge of a man's thoughts, beliefs or desires by anything else than by his words and actions.

It is a perfect truism to say that external conformity to a belief can be commanded; but that personal belief only exists, when the innermost judgment of a man is convinced by reasons; and that belief is only vigorous and effective when the desires and the will have set themselves in the same direction as the judgment. When Mr. Mallock says "that the moral end is inward, because it resides primarily not in action, but in motives to action, etc.," he says what every Positivist will agree to, in the same way as he would agree that the life of a plant was primarily in the seed and in the roots it sends into the ground. But Mr. Mallock has no such meaning as this for "inwardness." He seems to mean that it is better to think right than to do right, because God reads the thoughts and man can only see the actions.* So far this would seem to exonerate the Positivists from the terrible accusation of having been the first to assert that men could not see into each other's souls. But Mr. Mallock goes on to speak as if his real difficulty was to find a common ground of argument between the saint and the sinner. "Suppose that on positive grounds I find pleasure in humility, and my friend finds pleasure in pride, and so far as we can form a judgment the happiness of us both is equal, what possible grounds can I have for calling my state better than his?" (p. 99.)

None of course, if happiness be the only test of worth; any more than saying that a cane chair is preferable to a stuffed one, when two persons find themselves equally comfortable on either. Mr. Mallock gives us a very curious reason for making a choice. "Were I a Theist," he says, "I should have the best of grounds, for I should believe that hereafter my friend's present contentment would be dissipated, and would give place to despair." But how is the Theist able to demonstrate that pride belongs to the category of things which are destined to be followed in another world by despair? That would be the interesting and practical thing to know, and that is precisely what Mr. Mallock does not tells us. The Positivist

* "The moral end, then, is so precious in the mind of the Theist, because the inward state it consists of is agreeable to what God wills—a God who reads the heart and cannot be deceived." (p. 95.)

remark on this subject would be entirely unlike that which our author supposes. He would *not* be satisfied with knowing that a man might nourish pride, arrogance, and vanity all his life, whether that were mortal or immortal, and never, as the saying is, get out of conceit with them. But he would study this inward state of the heart in its origin; and finding this to consist of an estimate of personal self importance in obvious contradiction with real facts, Positivism would condemn these sentiments as absurd. Studying them further in their external consequences, in the habitual attitude of the man towards his fellows which they determine, Positivism finds these consequences to be in so many ways evil and anti-social, that it does not hesitate to condemn this state of heart, as not only absurd, but wicked, wicked in proportion to the intensity and development of the sentiments.

The final charge against the Positivists for this treatment of the moral law is, that according to them, "its value, such as it is, is measured only by the *conscious* happiness that its possession gives us, or the conscious pains that its loss gives us." (p. 100) Whereas to the Theist, whose "standard is God's will, not man's immediate happiness," "the issue [of the struggle between good and evil] is of an importance great out of all proportion to our own consciousness of the results of it." (p. 89) That is, of the *present* consciousness; but Mr. Mallock shows plainly enough that he believes the consequences of good or bad actions are to be considered exclusively from their effects upon the destiny of the person who performs them; not indeed in this world, but in some other. Unconsciousness of evil is only a temporary matter; it is certain that the veil will one day be torn away and the revelation made of the true state of things when the sinner is punished for them. Positivism on the contrary does not feel warranted in asserting that every man will always realize the consequence of his own actions, or even will always be punished for them in his own person. But it asserts that the good and evil of actions are so independent of "conscious happiness and conscious pains," that the frequently witnessed impunity of the wicked makes no difference in the enormity of the guilt, nor indeed of the moral suffering which he must experience if ever his eyes are opened. The Positivist indeed is deprived of the resource of the Catholic, whose blackest crimes may be washed away, redeemed, absolved, merely by the device of getting into a certain inward frame of mind which may leave unmodified all the consequences of those crimes, and all the misery they have inflicted upon other people. The Positivist cannot believe that sins which are scarlet shall ever be white as wool: and its powerful deterrent agency against wrong-doing, is the terrible conviction that it hardly ever can be undone; that the repentance, though sought bitterly and with tears, has rarely the opportunity to lift up the lives which may have been crushed, the hearts which may have been broken, or to restore the golden hours, days, or years which may have been darkened by injury.

Supposing that the man who has committed the injury does *not* repent, and supposing that, by exception, he happens to escape personal experience of the consequences of his evil doing, the Positivist doctrine will certainly have no influence over him. But, in this state of mind, neither will the Catholic. A man who will not learn to be sorry for having injured a fellow creature is certainly not likely to believe that he is to be sent to hell on account of this injury. Every one knows, moreover, that the Catholic sacraments of confession, and absolution, and extreme unction are arranged so conveniently to cover all sins with the least possible amount of specification or trouble of repentance, that a man would be a mere fool who should refuse to take such trouble, and yet fail to gratify himself with every thing he wanted and was able to procure. The logic of the doctrine is such that it may be safely asserted that the moralities which have developed and even flourished in the Catholic church, have done so not because, but in spite of doctrines, so clearly, often so odiously immoral.

What now becomes of the grand indictment against Positivism on the score of morality? This, it will be remembered, was under three heads. In the first place the Positivists are said to destroy the morality of the moral law, by denying as characteristic its essential attributes. In the second place it is alleged that they make of man an automatic part of nature, in whom actions result from physical or natural impulses, as involuntarily, as mechanically, and as irresistibly as a weather vane is blown towards the east by a wind coming from the west. To such a being it is absurd to attribute moral responsibility for actions which he cannot choose but commit. And finally, assuming that nothing exists but what science can demonstrate to the senses, "in other words, that the immaterial is the non-existent," Positivism claims to have destroyed the supernatural, and "by a mere dogmatic statement which can give no logical account of itself, but by which the modern world has been cowed," (p. 244), it has landed us in a "fatalism that will allow to us no moral being at all." (p. 255.)

We have seen, in opposition to this rhetorical accusation, that Positivism was no such impossible "materialism" as Mr. Mallock crudely supposes, or perhaps as he pretends to suppose it to be. That, as it accepts the testimony of consciousness as equally valid with the testimony of the senses, it has not the least idea of denying an "immaterial will," all the more as the conception of a "material will" is so nonsensical that it cannot for a moment be entertained. That *physical* science does not pretend to discuss the facts of consciousness or the laws of the operation of the will; but that *psychical* science does so, partly by methods borrowed from the physical sciences, partly by methods peculiar to itself. That the notions of a "supernatural agency arranging the molecules of the brain,"—of a self determining free will established like an innermost entity in the secret recesses of a supernatural entity, the soul,—are rejected, not because they are immaterial, but because neither the testimony of consciousness nor the testimony of the senses contain the slightest datum whence they may be inferred. That on the contrary it is believed that spontaneous activity, originating in the forces of an individual organism, is shown by observation to be the essential characteristic of a conscious individual, by which he is to be distinguished from an automaton. That in any individual sufficiently developed to possess a moral sense, this was found to constitute one of the permanent forces of the organism ; that the power of foreseeing the consequences of our own actions, is invariably accompanied by the power of modifying actions in accordance with such foresight ; therefore to any one endowed with a moral sense, actions invested with a moral character * and performed according to individual choice, are actions for which the individual is morally responsible, just as he is *neutrally* responsible for walking without a stumble when he has the normal power over his limbs, and the normal power of seeing an obstruction in the road. That the Positivist or natural sense of responsibility differs from the Mallockian or supernatural (?) in that it is not supposed to serve as an excuse either for some higher power to inflict a punishment, or for the

* Which, as seen, is not attributable to all actions, many of which are indifferent.

acting individual to find grounds for evading punishment; for such evasion was shown to be impossible, as all actions are followed by appropriate consequences, many of which are necessarily felt by the agent. In any case the consequences are felt in the Social Organism: and Positivist moral education constantly tends towards developing a state of mind and feeling, which should regard this social consequence as even more important than a personal one. Finally, to Positivism, the moral law is a complete elaboration of the social consciousness, studying human relations in their effects, immediate and remote, on social relations. Its judgments may in any given case be most precise and positive, and are always independent of individual designs; but they cannot be called absolute in any sense, since they are always relative to the nature and extent of the social relation involved.* Positivism lays stress on the necessity of the inward obedience of the heart to the moral law, since without this, external obedience is either false or uncertain; it demonstrates the importance of moral laws by tracing their connections with the fundamental conditions of social existence; it steadily endeavors to increase the influence of the social rewards and penalties which naturally attach to moral or immoral conduct, by intensifying the sense of community of interest with the social organism; and in so doing subordinates the conscious happiness or unhappiness which may result

* Catholicism offers an example of similar relativity, by its division into mortal sin and venial sin.

to each from his own conduct, to the wider question of the effects of this upon all.

From which it should appear, we think, that Positivism is very far from "destroying or paralyzing the faculty of moral judgment in us," although it refuses to call this judgment supernatural. And it certainly tends to eliminate nothing from that complex constitution of life, upon which is based such art as created Macbeth or the Antigone.

In stating that a certain development of social consciousness was required in order to make effective the most characteristic rewards and penalties which Positivism attributes to the moral law, we find ourselves again formally at issue with Mr. Mallock. He believes himself to have make the same statement in saying that the Positivists make sociology the foundation of morality; and believes also, that he has so effectually shown the absurdity of this foundation, that no one will be inclined to build on it any more. We have several times glanced at Mr. Mallock's conception of sociology; let us now examine it a little more in detail.

"The province of the sociologist," says our author, "within certain limits, is clear enough. His study is to the social body what the study of the physician is to the individual body. It is the study of human action as productive or non-productive of some certain general good." (p. 50.)

In this last sentence we find definitely stated the entire

misconception, equally unnecessary and profound, which vitiates all that Mr. Mallock has to say on the subject of sociology. A better understanding of his own simile might have saved him from error. For the study of the physician is directed towards seeing, *not* how any "general good" is to be evolved from the functions of the different organs of the body, but how these maintain its life and provide for its development. Similarly, sociology is the science of the social body or organism. It searches out its parts, ascertains their mutual relations or successive subordinations to one another, discovers their functions, demonstrates what conduces to the fulfilment of these functions, what, on the contrary, hinders and thwarts them; traces the line of progressive growth along which is arranged the series of its events, and by observation of that line, penetrates backwards towards its origin and forwards towards its probable future destinies. Sociology may be said to include the history, the anatomy, physiology, pathology and therapeutics of the social organism. It does not include its morals, because morality, derived from the mutual relations of elements *in* the organism, is an attribute of them and not of it.* In its definitions of the relations of these elements, it furnishes the fundamental data for the philosophy of the moral law; but this moral law is subsidiary to social science, and is enforced by public sentiment and public opinion. Similar-

* As osmosis is a phenomenon associated with the life of all the elements of our animal body, but evidently has nothing to do with that body as a whole.

ly sociology is *not* concerned with "general happiness," further than that this term is an expression for such nutritive well-being of the elements of society as may secure the proper performance of the functions of its organs. Mr. Mallock is right in considering this to be the "negative condition of happiness," not happiness itself. Happiness is a spontaneous result of the free play of the forces of life, or else is the creation of art, which, though deriving its data from the science of sociology, is necessarily independent of it, as art is always independent of science.

When, therefore, Mr. Mallock asserts, "The Positive school contend that it [the general good] is general happiness; and that there is the answer to the great question, What is the test of conduct and the true end of life?" he misrepresents the subject. If happiness be considered a test, it is as an ultimate and not as an immediate test of conduct. It is Catholicism, with its one promise of eternal felicity,—and not Positivism, which comes the nearest to proposing personal happiness as *the* aim of effort.

We have said already, "existence being the highest conceivable necessity, every thing which conduces to the extension of the largest existence involved, is good; every thing which tends to its diminution is an evil." Therefore Positivism applauds as leading to the "highest good" possible under the circumstances, many events which were productive of much individual misery. It applauds the heroic resistance of the Netherlands to Spain, notwithstanding sieges, and floods, and starvation of women and children. It applauds the emigration of the Puritans, though it led them into a wilderness of savage enemies, into hardships and pestilence and famine. It applauds the American civil war, though it strewed the land from the bayous of Louisiana, to the swamps of Chickahominy, with the flower of a nation's youth. To call such great social events productive of social happiness would indeed be absurd. But they all tended to a larger life; to the expansion of interests and energies that had been threatened with fatal repression; and, for reasons already stated, this expansion of social existence constituted a general good, to which individual happiness was justly subordinated.

The theory of Utilitarianism would indeed be as self-contradictory as Mr. Mallock tries to make it out, were it not for this conception of the needs of the social organism, with which individual needs must incessantly be compared. And it is impossible, as we have several times found occasion to insist, for anyone to have an adequate conception of the social organism, who does not understand the organic nature of individuals. In the physical part of these we find a constant subordination of individual cells to tissues, of tissues to organs; a constant interdependence of the functions of these upon one another. It is true that no healthy physical organism offers examples of the *sacrifice* of one part to another, or to the welfare of the whole, which is most complete when that of all the parts is perfect. Throughout the organic world however, we find such sacrifice entailed by the necessities of reproduction, which always involve greater or less disintegration of the individual, thus compelled to personal sacrifice for the sake of the race.* Other partial and temporary sacrifices of the body as a whole, become necessary, in order to secure larger advantages for that body, in proportion as the individual rises higher in the organic scale, and especially as he becomes endowed with the distinctively animal capacity of locomotion. Then, to secure food, or better and more abundant food, he is often compelled to submit to considerable fatigue and hardship, thus making his body suffer for the sake of his body. When in man, a deliberately conscious soul is added, still more imperious needs are awakened, to which the ease and even the needs of the body are often willingly sacrificed. Finally, these mental needs become subordinated to one another, not in any fixed order, but in varying ways according to the varying character of the individual. At the present stage of human development, few persons are equally conscious of all the needs of their moral nature; they sacrifice some to others unknowingly, and often unaware that they have made a sacrifice. The indolent man sacrifices his reputation to his sloth; the selfish sacrifices sympathy to greed; the violent defeats his own purposes for the gratification of

* It is well known that Mr. Spencer has insisted at length on the fact that reproduction always involves disintegration of parents.

avoiding restraint. Similarly the scholar and poet are ready to sacrifice health to their dreams, the statesman friendship to his ambition, and so on. The normal condition, if we may judge from the example of lower types, is the maintenance of such an equilibrium that no sacrifice should be required; but that all desires should be satisfied in due proportion, without excess and without privation.

But it seems probable that the close dependence of human satisfaction upon the social organism, and the extreme complexity of this makes the attainment of such equilibrium, or at least its maintenance for a long time, impossible. Hence the rise and development of the distinctively human capacity for voluntary sacrifice, known to be in a normal direction whenever the less is sacrificed to the greater, and not the reverse. Hence the honor which has gradually accrued to the spirit of self-sacrifice, as social honor inevitably tends to accrue to those known efforts which are at once difficult and necessary, which contradict primitive types, and thus the lowest instincts of human nature, but are needed for the completeness of the higher types, and thus for the complete development of the highest human nature. In this sense Mr. Mallock, echoing Dr. Bushnell, may say, "Gratification is natural; self-sacrifice is supernatural." The Positivist says: "The fulfilment of needs is according to nature; the sacrifice of needs for a higher purpose is according to human nature."

These are the considerations which show the irrelevance of Mr. Mallock's objections to the science of sociology, for the purposes for which he applies to it. "Its aim," he says, "is to produce health. Health is an important condition to the full enjoyment of anything, but it will by no means of itself give or guide us to the best thing. A man may be in excellent health, and yet, if he be prudent, be leading a degrading life. So too may a society. The cities of the Plain may, for all we know to the contrary, have been in excellent social health; indeed there is every reason to believe they were." *

* Mr. Mallock constantly betrays the feebleness of his own moral convictions by intimating that without morality, the world, though of course a very wicked place, might continue to be a very agreeable one. A well-known realistic writer, whom we should be far from willing to quote as an artist, but whose frequently disgusting pages, like Hogarth's horrible cartoons, may often render indirect service to morals, has given many powerful illustrations of the Positivist doctrine, that the reason for the importance of moral laws is the tendency to social dissolution consequent on their violation. As an offset to some of the luscious pictures quoted, not uncomplacently, by our author from Theophile Gautier, we would cite the following passage from *l'Assommoir*. It is the first occasion on which Coupeau comes home intoxicated, and reels into the laundry where his wife is at work:

"'Kiss me,' he said. 'You are a good woman.'

"As he spoke, he gave a sudden lurch, and fell among the skirts.

"'Do take care,' said Gervaise, impatiently, 'you will get them all mixed again.' And she gave him a little push with her foot, whereat all the other women cried out:

"'He is not like most men,' said Madame Putois. 'They generally wish to beat you when they come in like this.'

"Gervaise already regretted her momentary vexation, and assisted her husband to his feet, then turned her cheek to him with a smile, but he put his arm around her and kissed her neck. She pushed him aside with a laugh.

"'You ought to be ashamed,' she said, then yielded to his embrace. *And the long kiss they exchanged before these people, amid the sickening odor of the soiled linen and the alcoholic fumes of his breath, was the first downward step in the slow descent of their degradation.*" (Italics ours.)

Would not the "absolute rule" of Catholicism have rather justified this wifely submission?

We think examples less far-fetched, more to the purpose and more amenable to practical discussion, might have been selected than the semi-mythical cities of the Plain. However, the example is of minor importance. What *is* of importance is that the difficulty here, unlike that about hell, etc., is entirely of voluntary creation. Health, "including in the social organism sufficient wealth and freedom," may be enough to secure happiness or pleasure for a certain time, but no Positivist supposes that it necessarily secures either dignity or morals. The possibility of obtaining temporary happiness independent of these, results from the human range of choice within the sphere of its own activities, whereby these may be temporarily restrained much within the limits of their natural expansion. There is, however, a constant tendency to expansion; or, in other words, every human being has an inherent tendency to live his full life, and when a persistent voluntary limitation to certain parts of it, as, for instance, to sensual enjoyments, has destroyed the capacity for realizing this tendency, a profound misery is, sooner or later, the inevitable consequence. The blunder of the sensualist is that he seeks the infinity in the finite.

Nature has set a double bounds to his attempt: satiety, and the degradation and ruin of faculties, whose exercise is incompatible with his vices. It is on this account that they *are* vices, and it is contemplation of the results towards which they tend, that gradually generates moral repugnance for them, even when, by extreme prudence, these results will, in individual cases, be avoided. The moral taste is developed at least as slowly as any other, and all experience shows that until it *is* developed, the moral law, though preached with all the fervor of an apostle, is incapable of being practised with the inwardness and sense of supreme importance that Mr. Mallock justly claims for it.

It is, however, precisely such "impassioned and unselfish coöperation with the social law," which Mr. Mallock asserts to be impossible, "in the absence of any farther end to which the social law is to be subordinate." (p. 60.) The "farther end" which Mr. Mallock contemplates, is submission to the will of God. But as we have already seen, there is no way of ascertaining the will of God, supposing it to exist, except by study of its expression in the facts of the social organism, which are interpreted by the social law. Therefore if this "impassioned coöperation" be impossible under Positivism, it must be equally so under Theism.

Mr. Mallock thinks that "the fact in human nature on which the Positive school rely for their practical motive power," is the possession of sympathy and benevolence. "It is by these that the rules of social morality are to be absorbed and attracted into ourselves, and made the directors of all our other impulses. The feelings, however, that are thus relied on * * * are unequal in their distribution, partial and capricious in their action, and disturbed and counterbalanced by the opposite impulse of selfishness, which is just as much a part of our nature and just as generally distributed." (pp. 61 and 62.)

Mr. Mallock therefore returns to his original proposition that it is impossible to bring any motive to bear to influence the conduct of man in any particular direction, other than the threat that if they do not go in that direction they will infallibly go to hell.

It is evident from these remarks that Mr. Mallock supposes Positivism to expect that every human being submitted to the moral law, is to be capable of analyzing it to its elements, and of tracing its origin in such social necessities as we have exposed. But since all Catholics are not expected to understand the "recondite doctrines" which have been elaborated for their faith, all Positivists are not expected to philosophically analyse the doctrines which, if examined, would have been thus analysed for their understanding. Can no one obey the laws of health but physicians? Are we obliged to reflect on the processes of digestion every time we eat our dinner?

The art of living is necessarily based on the science of life. It is especially when failures in the art are threatened, that it is necessary to have recourse to the science, in order to explain the causes of such failures, and to find out if possible the means of averting them. Otherwise inquiry into the science, though of the highest speculative interest, and always to be made by all persons of calibre adequate to the task, is not practically essential.

The "motive force" of life is not reason, which, as Comte remarks, can only give light, but not force. The motive force is always a passion, active or latent; a passion appropriate to some special line of action, and, as we have seen, inevitably generated during the repetition of such actions. It sometimes is a sympathetic passion for the welfare of humanity; but quite as often it is something entirely distinct from this, even when the line of action it enforces has come to be considered right, because found to ultimately conduce to human welfare. Thus the sense of personal honor, susceptible of becoming a passion of the utmost intensity, and also of operating injuriously upon a certain segment of society, is, nevertheless, justly regarded as a moral sentiment, because on the whole, it is essential to every high character and to every high society. The man absorbed in it, may nevertheless, at any given moment, be the farthest in the world from thinking of sympathy or of benevolence.

It is the aim of Positivism, and of the moral education it designs, to bring the doctrine of the social organism, and of the organic relations of human beings, more and more vividly into the consciousness of mankind. Well aware of the feebleness of the sympathetic instincts, it attributes to their lack of development, or to their systematic perversion, a large part of the miseries and inadequacies, and disappointments which at present darken human life. It proposes therefore to develop such sentiments by every practicable means. It addresses those who are capable of speculation with the true philosophy of the doctrine, and confides to them the task of continually expounding and explaining it; of enforcing it by exhortation and illustration, by principle and by precept. Thus to the priests of Catholicism, Positivism opposes the philosophers. Over those unable to really understand ideas, it extends the influence of feelings, emotions, sentiments generated by ideas. It commands the ignorant, compels the vicious, trains the young and the weak. Positivism, in a word, proposes to do with its doctrine exactly what Catholicism has done with hers,—to extend it gradually but surely, over every department of human life; not as an arbitary unity, but as an organic power centralized in vitality, manifold in effects and application. Were the general appreciation of social relations to-day indefinitely further removed from the true standard than it is; were it as feeble and insignificant as Mr. Mallock asserts it to be; Positivism would be at least as much justified in preaching this central social doctrine now, as was Catholicism justified in preaching an ascetic purity, to a world that seemed absolutely incapable of understanding it.

From all this may be seen how completely erroneous is the supposition that "positive morality presupposes some one kind of happiness, which is open to all men, and which is better than all others;" (p. 44), some unique Prize of Life. This is exactly what Catholicism presupposes, and calls the prize eternal salvation. This salvation is so important that it not only surpasses all earthly interests, but theoretically and practically annihilates the majority of these altogether. Love, knowledge, sympathy, action, the delight of the eyes, the pride of life, these must be and have been effaced in the precise ratio of nearness of the portentous, unknown, unimaginable Prize, which loomed over earth from the heavens.

For this prize Positivism pretends to offer no equivalent. Nor does it, as Mr. Mallock supposes, identify the highest happiness with morality. Observance of moral laws is essential to the highest happiness, because essential to the largest development of life. But such observance is the means, not the end. A merchant does not go to sea in order to observe maritime law; but he observes the law in order to be able, with least let or hindrance, to go to sea. So a virtuous man does not live in order to practice virtue, but he practices virtue in order to be able to live, in the way which has come to be alone tolerable to him.

Happiness is the state of individual consciousness that, as a rule, occurs spontaneously, when all the powers of the individual are in equilibrium; when he is sufficiently occupied to keep his energies in tension without strain; when his thoughts and his sympathies have each an adequate object; when his imagination is supplied with an horizon, and his self-esteem with the possession of a social function. Happiness may occur or be created in the most various ways, like flowers, like poems like music. These spring from the inexhaustible richness of the universe of ideas and things, in which man finds himself immersed. As already hinted, the creations of art, even in its present more limited sense, of art of the beautiful, offer us the type of the freely created situations of delight, which it is the legitimate province of the human intellect to frame for the human soul. But these situations are as varying in number and character as are the souls that are to enjoy them. Mr. Mallock asks Prof. Huxley whether he "has ever enjoyed it [the highest happiness] himself, or whether he hopes to do so. If so, when and where and how? What must be done to get it, and what must be left undone; and when it is got, what will it be like?" (p. 40.) We have not the slightest doubt that Prof. Huxley could, if he chose, answer these questions very satisfactorily; but even his answer would not be unique, and when given would very likely prove unintelligible to Mr. Mallock.

The nearest "common happiness" in which we may all "become partakers," is a delight in life—in life for its own sake, hence a delight in everything that ministers to it, or develops it, or explains it. This delight has always existed, but it is unequally divided, and it is capable, in many places at least, of immensely greater development.

The classification of "goods" or happinesses as pleasures is, as Mr. Mallock has justly remarked, "traversed" by another, in which the good which is a pleasure, may become subordinated to a good which is a pain. We have already said that this peculiar feature in human life was due to its extreme complexity, which rendered the maintenance of perfect equilibrium so difficult as to be impossible, and constantly necessitated therefore alternative of sacrifices. A common measure for the "good," however, may still be found—found, as hitherto, in the Positivist doctrine—in the conditions of existence. The greater effort implies the greater expenditure of vital force. The effort of self-sacrifice is so great that, when made for a worthy object, it ranks higher than almost any other. The self-sacrifice of a peasant girl may involve a greater relative expenditure of vital force than the intellectual effort of a scholar—certainly involves far more than the passive reception of pleasure, on the part of a sybarite. It is in this way that the moral world is brought to a level with the intellectual world, and both are raised above the world of enjoyment, in itself so legitimate. *There is no such thing as a unique and common happiness; there is only a common measure of value and dignity, found in the degree of vital effort expended in the attainment of each good that is recognized as a happiness.*

Having reached this point in our examination of Mr. Mallock's essay, and of his accusation against Positivism as something which, unchecked, is destined to plunge the world into "mindless desolation," we are compelled to pause and answer the question which may have been latent in the minds of certain readers.

This question is, Why have we taken so much trouble to controvert the positions assumed in this liveliest of philosophical disquisitions? For, whatever merit or demerit the book may have, there can be no question that it is extremely lively, and, under the circumstances, this attribute of liveliness is liable to be a very dangerous one. It is calculated to attract, and is undoubtedly intended to attract, the very persons who are most liable to be imposed upon by its show of argument; whose ignorance of Positive thought and of the method of physical science is even greater than Mr. Mallock's, and who, therefore, are quite unable to control his innumerable misstatements. Persons moreover who have lost faith in theology, who are no adepts in metaphysics, who, from absence of training, experience a great deal of difficulty in appreciating the full significance of the Positivist doctrine, and yet who are extremely ill at ease for lack of some general system of ideas which they do not know where to find. These are the persons to whom Mr. Mallock refers, in a remark of which he is evidently proud, for he quotes it from one of his own essays: "People cannot be always exclaiming in drawing-rooms that they have lost their Lord, and the fact may be temporarily forgotten because they have lost their portmanteau. * * * There are many about us, though they never confess their pain, and perhaps themselves hardly like to acknowledge it, whose hearts are aching for the religion that they can no longer believe in." (p. 201.) Now this class of people, for we are far from denying that they exist, are liable to a certain cold shiver, an inward heart-quake, when they listen to Mr. Mallock's dismal and confident prophecies of what will happen if Positivism is allowed to succeed. When told that the moral life will probably in literal truth,

> "Creep on a broken wing,
> Through cells of madness, haunts of horror and fear;"

that "conscience will remain * * * as the menacing ghost of the religion which [Positivism] has murdered;" that if the "dawning self-consciousness [of man] contains that negation* of the supernatural which our positive assertions are at present supposed to necessitate, that then * * * this last development of humanity * * * will be the sort of break which takes place when a man awakes from a dream, and finds all that he most prized vanished from him;" that then "this discovery by man of himself will be the beginning of his decadence: it will be the discovery on his part that he is a lesser and lower thing than he thought he was, and his condition will sink till it tallies with his own opinion of it;"—when, we say, the readers we are thinking of are told all these things, it is small wonder if they are alarmed. Far less terrible threatenings would suffice to awaken that instinct of con-

* Does Mr. Mallock's self consciousness "contain a negation" of the Delphic oracle, in which nevertheless, we presume he does not believe?

servatism, that vague dread of the unknown, latent in the majority of English bosoms, perhaps in the greater number of human hearts. Everyone knows the excitement, half rage, half terror, which has been caused by the theory of the descent of man from apes. If such a sense of ignominy can be felt on account of the condition of our remotest ancestors, whose limitations we unquestionably have outgrown, it is not astonishing that the anticipation of future degradation, much less remote, would fill the souls of those entertaining it with despair. Those who shiver at the thought, that, at a distance of centuries, their great-grandfathers might have been gibbering monkeys, can hardly fail to be still more disconcerted at the prospect of seeing their own children converted into "wallowing pigs." And, under the pressure of vague alarms and the influence of "sounding phrases," they are not unlikely to flock to Mr. Mallock or to his confessor with the cry, "What shall we do to be saved?"

There are three reasons why this possibility fills *us* with an alarm, which is very far from vague. The first is that the answers given by these gentlemen are untrue. The second, that they are powerless for the purpose for which they are designed. The third, that they stand in the way of the appreciation, both of the real difficulties of the present situation and of the real remedies for them.

To show why we think the answers given by Mr. Mallock are untrue would be to rewrite the foregoing pages. It will be sufficient here to recall the outline of the argument. That Mr. Mallock's accusations of the "degrading" tendencies of Positivism repose on two untenable assertions. First, that Positivism "unifies the apparent dualism of things," denies immaterial feelings, thoughts, ideas, principles, volitions, simply because they cannot be seen or touched, and changes man from a "moral being" to an automatic machine, with conscious appetites but no conscious personality. Second, that *even if this were not so*, morality, dignity and enjoyment are rendered impossible in human life so soon as human beings are not supposed to live forever, and so soon as they are not supposed to be gazed upon by a Superhuman Being who created them. The first of these assertions was shown to be in flat contradiction to the Principles of Positivism, which accepts from consciousness testimony in regard to the immaterial world, in the same way as it accepts from the senses evidence about the material world, and which considers the researches of physical science into this material world, chiefly as the indispensable preliminary to a philosophy of morals and of social life, based, not upon tradition or upon assertion, but upon real analysis of the elements derived from consciousness which enter into them.

The second assertion, involving, not a question of fact, but a matter of opinion, was contradicted by an appeal to experience. This showed that the moral law, however professing to depend on a divine command, was really always evolved by experience, in the same way as any other law, and derived its profoundest sanctions from the accumulated knowledge of the effects of actions, and intensified emotions generated during the acquisition of such knowledge. That no authenticated means of finding out the will of God had ever existed, except study of the universe, he was supposed to have established. That the interests which have really animated human life have always been contained within itself. Even the pleasures and profits of proselytism and conversion, though directed professedly towards another world, have fully realized all their satisfactions in this one. The fear of another world has indeed often succeeded in making this life uncomfortable, miserable, wretched to the highest degree, but the hope has rarely exercised much influence except in the fury of battles,* or at those moments of transcendental heroism which Mr. Mallock himself insists must be of rare occurrence.

It is absolutely impossible that man can be made "an animal of far fewer capacities," (p. 161) merely by becoming fully imbued with the Positive view of himself; since upon any hypothesis a hope of heaven cannot create, but merely direct a capacity. If this hope be taken away, therefore the capacity is not annihilated, but turned in other directions.

---

* The influence of the hope of Paradise in exciting military ardor is so much more conspicuous than its influence in any other direction, that it might be adduced as another illustration of the close connection existing between the theological and the military spirit.

The largest existence ever really contemplated by human thought is humanity, and the divine attributes which were supposed to constitute objects of contemplation, are really all derived from this. Whatever sense of dignity might be conferred by the belief that human life was gazed upon and ordered by an unknown Supreme Being, is fully equalled by the dignity of feeling that this same human life constitutes a real part of the most Supreme Being known.

We have endeavored further to show that Mr. Mallock's argument for Theism, professes to be based upon demonstration, not of its truth, but of its utility. That nevertheless, at the very climax of this reasoning, he turns suddenly round and announces that Theism, though useful as furnishing reasons for rendering human life interesting and momentous, is really far from giving a logical explanation of even its most obvious facts; that it is useless as a practical guide, and theoretically, only serves to suggest speculative mysteries which are eternally insoluble and unintelligible. Theism is thus worse than Positivism, unless a special revelation of the divine will be added to its fundamental dogma. No attempt is made by Mr. Mallock to prove either that *any* such supernatural revelation has been given, or to decide between the conflicting claims of rival revelations. He merely remarks that, *the necessity of revelation once admitted*, the Christian revelation must to western minds evidently bear off the palm of supremacy. *This* conceded, it is further evident that Protestant Christianity must be thrown aside, because destitute of the primary qualification which makes any revelation desirable, namely, a claim to infallibility. That this claim as made by the Catholic church is, on the contrary, so consistent with this *a priori* necessity of infallibility, that it must be at once admitted as just; and with it all the dogmas of the Catholic theology; that none of these need "stagger us," because they are not any more difficult to understand than other things which we do not hesitate to pronounce true. "Simplicity is no test of truth."

This last dictum is perfectly true. But the important circumstance in Mr. Mallock's logic is, that *no* test of truth is considered necessary. Having vehemently denounced certain persons who he thinks are trying to make moral truth a matter of individual taste, he yet does not hesitate to advocate a principle which must make *all* truth a matter of individual convenience and caprice. His doctrine is, "Whatever seems comfortable for the moment, is to be believed, for there can be no other office for belief than that of making human hearts comfortable." Mr. Mallock says that "Prof. Huxley will only be laughed at and not listened to, if he proclaims his own taste in sweetmeats with all the thunders of Mt. Sinai." (p. 122.) But he fails to tell how *his* own tasts for sweetmeats,—and sweetmeats of the most luscious and least nutritive kind, is to be commended to any one who has rather a robust preference for beefsteak.

We believe that Mr. Mallock flatters Positivism when he attributes to it exclusively a sense of the importance of truth. Every system of thought, theological, metaphysical, philosophic, has always insisted on such importance, so long as it was conscious of enough vital vigor to defend its own claims to be the sole interpreter of truth. No surer sign of conscious decrepitude could be imagined than this device of modern religiosities, to evade laborious search after truth by pretending that truth is unnecessary. Mr. Mallock conceals this stigma of decrepitude by an air of vivacity, which, like the lively gestures of an old coquette, can only deceive at a distance. He calls "devotion to truth as truth," the "last resource" of the Positivists. He upbraids these for wishing to hold to truth at all hazards, and in spite of its consequences; he ridicules the idea of applying "ethical adjectives," as "sacred" and "lofty" to any such truths as the Positivists can concern themselves with; or "heroic" to the most self-sacrificing efforts made to discover and establish them. He alleges various examples to show that "the truths that it is sacred to find out and to publish are not all truths, but truths of a certain kind only," (p. 153), an exquisitely Jesuitical doctrine. "A man discovers that his wife has been seduced by his best friend. Is there any thing very high or very sacred in that discovery? Having made it, does he feel any consolation in the knowledge that it is the entire truth? and will the gladness of true heroism visit him if he proclaims, it to everyone in his club? A chattering nurse betrays his danger to a sick man. Was the discovery of the truth of his danger very glorious for the patient, or was its publication very sacred in the nurse?" (p. 153.) Such are the examples which Mr. Mallock adduces as parallel to the vast questions of the significance of human life, and of its relations to powers within or without it!

"Thus," he concludes, "his [the Positivist's] devotion to truth, if it mean anything, and the language he often uses about it betrays this, let us know the worst, not let us find out the best: a wish which is neither more nor less noble than the wish to sit down at once in a slop upon the floor rather than sustain oneself any longer above it on a chair that is discovered to be rickety." (p. 160.)

We might notice that the courage to know the worst is generally accompanied by a resolution to fight for the best attainable. That not Positivists alone would regard as a mark of childish weakness, a deliberate choice of false security in preference to real knowledge of a real situation, which must, sooner or later, make itself known. And that the indolent fool in Mr. Mallock's wilfully ignoble simile, who, to avoid wetting his feet, would cling to a rickety chair for support, really deserves to fall to a much lower depth than "a slop on the floor."

But we are not sorry Mr. Mallock has chosen this simile of a rickety chair. We believe that it does indeed well symbolize the kind of moral support which to-day may be afforded by the worn-out dogmas of Catholicism.

We are far from believing that the love of truth, more than any other virtue, is innate in the human breast or even springs eternal there. It is gradually developed from three sources, each the experience of a special necessity. These are, the necessity for confidence in the mutual relations of human beings, which develops the sense of honor towards men; the necessity that anything which is done or made should really be what it proposes to be,—source of integrity in work; finally, the necessity of understanding the real relations towards ourselves of a world with which we are incessantly coming into relation,—source of desire for reality in knowledge.

Thus honor, integrity and science, derived from different aspects of human relations, converge to a single sense of truth, that tends to become the more sacred the more human life is seen to depend upon it. No Pontius Pilate jests at truth when it concerns the efficacy of the medicines which are to bring his son from the brink of the grave. No Sunday-school regrets the exactitude with which a mineralogist may have determined the line of cleavage of crystals, when upon the precision of this knowledge may depend the safety of the bridge to be crossed by its picnic party. The knowledge of the unforeseen effects of knowledge or of ignorance, which has only been really obtained in modern times, is the reason that in these times the feeling about truth has intensified from a lukewarm acquiescence, to a powerful passion, which, in the final stage of its development, is able to detach itself from the original utilities and exist for its own sake; is able to become an end, a satisfaction in itself, and, as Mr. Mallock justly remarks, an immense resource of modern life. Science unquestionably arose from the need of inquiring into the nature of the things which man wished to use. But at the present day, a true scientist would hold that science was belittled if limited to obvious or even to remote utilities; that knowledge is to be acquired in order to enable us to know; that "the solution of every problem suggests new questions to be solved,"* and that the highest and most permanent usefulness of scientific truth is in the inexhaustible field of activity it offers to the human intellect.

But how does this differ from the old consecrated assertion that the final occupation of the human race was to be the contemplation of the divine perfection? For where are these to be found displayed except in the works of the creation?

Thus if it ever be possible for a virtue, acquired in the course of social evolution, to "become primary," it certainly would be the virtue of truth. It is essential to action, it is indispensable to thought, and for those who make the development of thought the practical business of their lives, the desire of truth for its own sake is reinforced by a sense of honor towards fellow creatures who are to depend upon them for finding it out. They do

* Stanley Jevons, loc. cit.

not dare to decide which truths are useful and important and which may be neglected, for to do this would be to make of their own fallible opinion the arbiter of human destinies. For art, it is permitted to select, to choose; but for science, for reality, for what is to form the basis of a philosophy of life, no knowledge of life may safely be omitted, no laborious precision of detail be considered superfluous.*

The great Positivist doctrine about truth is, that it is always an expression of relations existing between the human mind and the object that is contemplated by it. Things are not known in themselves, but only as they affect us and as we can perceive them. What is true for us is what we see to be true, and any other truth is inconceivable by our minds. But as we are only concerned in the relations of things to ourselves, the most perfect expression of truth for us means the most comprehensive and exact statement of these relations. Thus the highest truth necessarily coincides with the widest utility.

This, as we have already hinted, is the elementary philosophy of the text-books, to-day almost everywhere admitted in place of the ancient ontological speculations, or researches into the nature of Being. But that this doctrine, or else its consequences, are not universally or

* We think there is a profound philosophical error in the claim so often made at the present day, that because science must be universal, art must be realistic, and may be enjoined to copy, not only the true, but the ugly and the repulsive.

completely understood, even by the nations whose philosophers have been the foremost to establish it, is shown by this extraordinary attempt of as popular a writer as Mr. Mallock, to prove that there can be a higher utility than truth, and to demonstrate that belief on the most important subjects can and should repose on something else than demonstration.

The plausibility of this attempt is derived from a circumstance which thinkers have no right to take into account, but for which those who desire to practically influence public opinion must make wide allowance. This is the inability of the mass of people to think, and their correlative liability to be led by emotional considerations *from* anything which seems either tedious or alarming, and towards anything which seems piquant and attractive. It is to these people, and not to thinkers, that Mr. Mallock's essay is addressed. Any one who has once become accustomed to ask as first question, "Is it true?" becomes immediately indifferent when told, "It is not exactly true, but, etc., etc." So when Mr. Mallock slips in, almost as if it were some legal technicality designed to protect himself against possible injunctions, the remark, "as to the *proof* of all this, we may as well admit, at least provisionally, that there is none," persons accustomed to seek truth for a foundation, cannot fail to be irretrievably repelled from further interest in the matter. They feel themselves in the position of a capitalist who should have been invited to invest a fortune in building a block of houses in the clouds. "Only a single jump," says the subscription agent, with a persuasive wave of the hand, "and you are there; and the first stone once laid, the whole structure rises almost of itself."

"Like an exhalation" adds the man of substance, and declines to invest. But how shall those who are not men of substance regard this beautiful structure of clouds? How shall they learn to detect the unwholesome fens, the stagnant marshes, the pestilential swamps, that have bred these watery vapors, which glitter for a moment so brilliantly while tinged by a roseate fancy or by the violet of a languishing imagination?

Indeed we hardly know; and it is experience of the tenacity with which the forces of imagination and affection cling to old ideals, the reluctance with which, at the bidding of reason, they attach themselves to new, that convinces us that the "complete triumph of Positivism" is much farther off than Mr. Mallock fears. It is useless to build a house on the most solid foundations, with the strongest walls, the noblest over-arching roof; the human soul stands shivering on the threshold, and will not enter in to take possession until it has been completely furnished; until its ceilings have been dimmed by clustered associations, and its hearth-stones have become browned by many fires. And yet, with its old dwelling places masses of crumbling ruins, not burned, but worm-eaten with gradual decay, where is the poor, roofless soul to find shelter?

Not, we energetically protest, within those ancient sanctuaries, picturesque as ruins, but deadly as habitations. The remedy for languor and weakness is *not* the transient stimulant of half sensuous excitement, which quickens the pulse for a moment, only to leave the real prostration more profound. The only remedy for weakness, is the severe, strenuous, unrelenting cultivation of strength. We believe indeed that the thorough and logical acceptance of Positivism necessitates immensely more strength than belief in Catholicism: we believe that the rise of the Positivist doctrine, is an important evidence of that "expansion of human powers," which Mr. Mallock thinks so incredible; but we are convinced also, that it works steadily for their constant expansion, while the essential crime of Catholicism is in its ceaseless efforts for their repression. The Positivist doctrine nourishes the strength it demands; the Catholic, perpetuates the weakness it offers to sustain, and eternalizes the woes it promises to comfort.

Is there no reality in these woes? Is there no prospect of difficulty or of danger, peculiar to modern times which may justify notes of warning? Have any such great changes recently taken place in the conditions of human life, as may give an entirely "new import" to the question of its value and significance? What situation does Mr. Mallock really have in view, when he announces a "practical prospect" of listlessness, weariness, indifference, ennui and desolation; prospect of a time when prudent sensuality shall have replaced dangerous vice; where the general diffusion of well-being shall have removed all reason for self-sacrificing virtue; and the facile attainment of material comforts shall deprive exertion of its ancient stimuli of want and privation?

This is no imaginary picture; nor does it belong to a near or distant future, to dawn upon us with the triumph of Positivism. It is rather a photograph of a sufficiently extensive portion of the "upper classes" in the modern world: a tableau vivant, whose dramatis personæ are ornaments in many of the luxurious drawing-rooms which Mr. Mallock evidently frequents, and doubtless also adorns.

It is very noticeable in studying Mr. Mallock's pages, and the rhetoric which borders them,—often as irrelevant to the purpose as the illuminations of a missal to its text,—that the great, the real, the portentous danger he apprehends, is that of ennui. We feel constantly that he has been often immeasurably, horribly bored; that he has seen innumerable fellow-creatures, well dressed, well fed, in good health, without a ripple of anxiety on the surface of their lives, yet suffering so much from boredom that their existence was a burden to them. We feel that Mr. Mallock is as exclusive in his preference for good, even titled company, as ever was our dear old Miss Edgeworth; that the tears he sees shed are invariably dried by the finest of cambric handkerchiefs; that the brows he knows to ache are moistened with the best eau de cologne;

that the delicate and indiscribable sufferings of which he may have been the confident, have been detailed in cushioned armchairs, wheeled near oriel windows, sunk in endless depths of luxurious stillness, calm and repose. We know that our author has observed with sympathy the decorous dulness in which herds of well-bred women pass their days; he has seen them sigh furtively over their embroidery; he has seized the propitious moment, and offered them an altar cloth instead. He has seen young men, rich, well educated, emasculated for lack of some worthy object of ambition, sink passively into stupid dissipations. To some of these perchance, on the morning after a debauch, he has suggested the attractions of the cross and the excitements of a new Catholic crusade. He has been listened to with interest; he has seen young eyes lose their unnatural languor and sparkle with youthful hope, fire and energy; he has known young hearts cease to sicken with a vague disease; and the same melancholy of adolescence which he has told us that Mr. Mill learned to terminate in one way, he, to the glory of the church, succeeds in obliterating in another. Mr. Mallock has studied the natural conditions of human life exclusively in the examples of those who live in unnatural conditions; and then concludes that, at the very moment Positivism is about to make a greater demand upon the resources of the world "than ever before," the world has become less able than ever to respond to it. And, as we write, it occurs to us that this circumstance is another point of resemblance between Mr. Mallock and the Emperor Julian, with whom we began to compare him. Julian also, from the uppermost heights of Roman society, was unable to appreciate the condition of the vast strata of human beings lying below; nor did he really understand the nature of the forces which were upheaving these strata into new combinations. The ancient gods, the fair temples, the philosophic nobleness and calm sufficed for him, and sufficed also to disgust him with the unintelligible pretensions of the Nazarene and of the rabble which followed him. We should be glad to believe that the content of Mr. Mallock, as of his leader Father Newman, with their revival of antique faith, were really as profound and sincere as we do not doubt that of the more famous apostate to have been.

So long as social progress is supposed to consist exclusively in the increase of material comfort, the anomaly must continue to confront us, that the very people who are the most comfortable, should be, habitually, the most discontented. The anomaly is only to be explained when the search for a prize to life is precluded by a scientific inquiry into the nature of the persons competing for it. "You must be able," says Mr. Mallock, "to say what *I* shall have, and I, and I." This is, in a measure, true, or will be true if our science of human nature be found, on inquiry, to be sufficiently advanced to answer the preliminary question, "What am I capable of wanting, and I, and I?"

We have said several times—since Mr. Mallock has asserted the contrary several times—that the prize of life, considered as happiness, is *not* morality, which only furnishes the negative conditions of happiness. Neither is it religion, which, with few exceptions, has always been looked upon as furnishing the police force by which these negative conditions could be regulated. It is only when morality and religion have become the motive powers for effort, that they can be thought of as more closely associated with happiness, since the expenditure of force in successful effort always engenders a happy state of consciousness in the person exerting himself.

The prize of life, or the object of living for each living being, consists in the development of all faculties to their greatest extent which the individual organization admits of, and in the satisfaction of all desires to their utmost possible capacity. The reason for failure and discontent will always be found in the fact, not that a "supernatural" stamp has been effaced, like a spurious watermark, from things which have been valued, but in the fact that some of these valued things have not been obtained, or that an imperfect analysis of the needs of human nature has caused the necessity for certain provisions for attainment to be overlooked.

For if, instead of relying on fantastic dogmatisms, we appeal to observation, what do we find as causes of human discontent, listlessness and weariness? On the one hand, millions ground down by unremitting toil: on the other hand, thousands pining in inactivity. Here men worn prematurely gray by anxiety; there others, prematurely wilted by debaucheries sought to relieve the tedium of days too free from anxiety. On this side mothers to whom maternity has become a burden; on that side, virgins to whom childlessness is a curse. Minds uselessly strained by responsibilities too many for them, and minds cruelly compressed into duties far too narrow. Energies that can find no employment, and work which remains undone in dearth of adequate energies. Households desolated by untimely deaths, and communities pauperized by untimely births. Sham art and shallow science justified on pretext of the claims of industry, and successful industry, unwieldy and over fat, unable to procure enjoyment through its abject ignorance of science and art. Mankind slaving like a spider, which spins eternally from its own bowels, yet starving in hideous misery in the midst of the riches its ceaseless labors have created. Love pampered and despised, worshipped, yet turned out of doors—pretext for the gilded belittlement of the half of the human race it most frequently ruins; love thwarted, fettered, throttled by a thousand things which are not love, or else drowned in dissolute slime. Belief become impossible in nerveless souls that have slipped through the chains of authority, yet find themselves unable to stand alone; incapable of energetic conviction, because not daring to act in accordance with their convictions; incapable of rooting themselves in a purpose, and therefore indifferent to the truth essential to the success of a purpose. There is a sense in which it is profoundly true that all personal and social ills may be summed up in the lines:

> But ill for him who, bettering not with time,
> Corrupts the strength of heaven-descended Will,
> And ever weaker grows thro' acted crime,
> Or seeming-genial venial fault,
> Recurring and suggesting still!
> He seems as one whose footsteps halt,
> Toiling in immeasurable sand,
> And o'er a weary, sultry land,
> Far beneath a blazing vault,
> Sown in a wrinkle of the monstrous hill,
> The city sparkles like a grain of salt.

Let us take a typical human life as it may be already imagined—and as it already not unfrequently exists. A child, well born and well nurtured, with healthy powers unfolding unthwarted, through the Paradise of infancy, cherished in the deep nest of family affection. A youth, securing the delight of vigorous training for faculties of body and soul, whose possession is itself a thrill of delight, led into the inexhaustible realm of knowledge of himself, of his race, of the universe, from thence to select the special equipment for his own career. A man or woman, freely choosing such career from among the innumerable possibilities of social activities, and feeling the first flush of life deepen with the conscious exertion of strenuous energies. A friend tasting the subtle and varied charm of comradeship in action, sympathy in feeling, companionship in life. A lover adding to the charm of friendship, the glowing force of a mysterious passion. A parent, converging upon a new life all the powers, the riches, the memories, the hopes of his own. A citizen, mingling in the tumult of social existence, sharing its responsibilities, contributing to its maintenance, furthering its progress, ameliorating its miseries, aiding its creations. A philosopher beginning to step aside from the current, with vital energies stored up in riches as fossil forests in coal, to be given out again in new forces, finding in the contemplation of the vast movement of the world, or of the smaller eddies near him, sufficient compensation for the slackening in the impetus of his own life.

Upon this bare outline of destiny, the natural inheritence of every human being, let us recall the the innumerable combinations of elements, which make up the depth and body of color of the picture. Let us remember how sentiment enriches energy, and how ambition may intensify or compensate for love. How knowledge may redound to personal profit, or social sacrifice become a personal career. How pleasures of the senses make a setting for the delights of the soul, and how the spiritual life may be so intense as, for a while, to efface all consciousness of the senses. How the love of beauty may become a passion, and the love of knowledge lead where the hope of heaven itself has been insufficient to prevent recoil. How strange and special affinities develop themselves between the tiniest parts of the universe of things, and the human minds attached to them, so that they can live on them and in them as tenaciously as limpets on a rock. How strange and unforseen delights spring up in the midst of calamities, like flowers in the depths of a morass. How in the conflict with evil, such good is experienced as if the evil itself had been transmitted into good. How the personal pleasures are multiplied in social intercourse, as light is refracted in a prism; and how personal happiness is intensified in the effort to procure it for other people, as the face of a man answers himself in a mirror. How the joy of animal living is ennobled by the consciousness of the social function which lifts the man so far above the animals. How the "insoluble problem" of the coexistence of good and evil is solved, by seeing that they insensibly pass into each other; that they are the relative excess or deficiency of each other, and thus necessarily coeternal. That it is therefore impossible to imagine a world so good that no evil will remain to be combated, or so evil that no good can be found to continue existence. Perfection is not the attribute of a future state, be that a utopia or the millennium; it can only exist in moments, but in jewelled moments which are strewn like diamonds throughout the "depths of space and time."

Upon this sketch of a human life, successful enough to be generally regarded as desirable, Mr. Mallock would make the criticism that, after all, it does not amount to anything. Indeed he has made this criticism already; it is the point of departure of his entire essay, the express reason for writing it. The criticism more often and more rationally made is, that this type of living is so rarely realized; that the regular evolution of life is so often thwarted: its legitimate satisfactions denied: its hopes disappointed: its plans ruined: its powers weakened by mental and bodily illness: its original character degraded; and above all, that all life is constantly darkened by the shadow of death, by the untimely snatching away of the lives with which it is so closely associated; by its own too early close at the very moment of fruition.

In regard to an immense number of the evils which afflict mankind and diminish the desirableness, if not the value of life, modern thought *has* given an entirely "new import" or significance. It has ceased to look upon them as chastisements of either just or petulant gods, or to assume for them a providential intention of discipline. Even when profiting by the discipline which strenuous struggle with difficulties affords, the Positivist deplores the waste of energies, most cruel when unsuccessful, but always as cruel as is the waste of life expended in gaining a battle. But he never ceases to look upon the evils as horrors, destined to be outgrown spontaneously, or to be overcome by courageous effort guided by real knowledge. Catholicism means submission to a world inherently evil, and which can only be rendered tolerable by constant meditation upon flight from it. Positivism means mastery of a world, naturally imperfect, but tending towards indefinite progress, and destined to submission to the intellect of man, who is to dwell in it. Positivism is far from fostering that passive acquiescence in spontaneous improvement which Mr. Mallock assumes to be the only logical result of a theory of progress. For it recognizes that, beyond a certain stage of development, changes in human destiny depend immediately upon the combined knowledge, desire and will of human beings, —and the energies of Positive thought are directed towards modifying these with so much the more intensity that they are inspired by assured hope of success.

It is one of the many silly assumptions that abound in Mr. Mallock's essay, that the efforts of Positivism, and the value of physical science in the amelioration of human life, are expended exclusively upon the attainment of physical comforts. We have already had occasion to notice several ways in which the influence of physical science transcended the material objects with which it might be immediately concerned. The influence upon happiness is not less remarkable. To the degree to which it has dissipated the mysteries enshrouding the material world, physical science has dispelled fear, and the slavish habits bred of fear. To the degree to which it has procured relief from physical pain, physical science has quickened compassion and engendered sentiments of humanity. By the same influence it has developed an intolerance of suffering which, if sometimes leading to effeminate shrinking from exposure, is as often and more markedly felt in the determination aroused to remove suffering even at the expense of personal sacrifice and danger,—felt also in a constantly increasing sensitiveness to conditions accepted during ignorance, but becoming intolerable with every advance in knowledge. The greatest of evils—death—remains, and the fact that Positivism neglects the doctrine of immortality, by means of which the evil of death is supposed to be mitigated, suffices to condemn it in the eyes of an immense number of people. Positivism however questions whether, at the present day at least, the doctrine of immortality does to any serious extent mitigate the pain of death. At the time its influence is most required—by a recent grave—the doctrine can be only a hope. But if ten or twenty years roll by, and the moment draws near when the hope may be realized in fact, the horrible pain it has been needed to assuage, has, in the immense majority of cases, subsided. In reality it is not death which is an evil, but premature and useless death. Such are the deaths occurring daily by the million, due to the most ignominious or trifling accidents, mark of the brutal triumph of blind forces as yet unsubjugated by reason and knowledge. For these deaths the only consolation is, that in the present imperfect condition of things death compensates as much evil as it creates. It is therefore far from useless. But when we remember that the natural term of human life is probably from eighty to a hundred years, it is evident that at present, death is nearly always premature.

Were no one born into the world, for whose maintenance suitable provision had not been made; and did no one die except of old age, abject poverty and the terror of death, the two greatest of existing evils, would be annihilated. "The last enemy to be destroyed is death." But until this victory—already conceivable, though so immensely remote—be achieved, we believe that the hope of reunion with the beloved dead can hardly fail to keep alive some form of belief in a life after death.

It is therefore possible that the personal happiness anticipated by Positivism, be only of such a kind "as has been many times experienced already," and not something so new, and vague, as to be "sounding," but quite "unthinkable." Positivism does not desire the sounding brass and tinkling cymbal, to be strummed in front of a curtain whose rising is always promised but constantly postponed. It boldly claims the real music, which it knows may be created by those who have really mastered the science of harmony. When Mr. Mallock asks us "what do you want from Life?" We answer, "Everything that the experience of thousands of years shows that it has in store for us," and when he further says, "what does your altruistic sentiment impel you to seek for your fellow-man?" We answer, "Everything which we ourselves desire, and that he is able to receive."

In the above outline of life, which we believe may at least fitly parallel Mr. Mallock's culmination of existence at the feet of a tinsel and plaster madonna, is implied the constant presence of one condition, which however is not by any means always present. We mean a certain state of tension; some consciousness of imperative necessity, of strenuousness in the exercise of faculties. This is sufficiently provided in average lives, by the presence of the difficulties, which so often threaten their ruin. These difficulties are so widely distributed, that no one, adequately conscious of social existence as a whole, can fail to feel their pressure,—however smooth may be the progress of his own personal career. In the absence of such social consciousness, exceptionally fortunate lives become abnormally free from a sense of tension,—or of struggle against difficulties. This is the cause of the listlessness and ennui of the so-called "upper classes" of modern societies. The members of these classes who do not personally submit to any external pressure of circumstances, and whose horizon is bounded by the outline of their own lives, are, practically, unaware of the pressure weighing in excess upon other parts of the social organism. They may know, as a curious or pitiful fact that such pressure exists: but as it has no effect upon their own actions, it can have no effect upon their own feelings. They are unconscious that they are really part of a living organism, which suffers: they believe that they are set apart, by fortune or providence, to enjoy. Whether or no enjoyment will ever be the unique occupation of human beings,—it is certain that it can never normally constitute the exclusive occupation of one class until it does so of all. For as we have seen, occupation is part of the nutrition of the organic elements of society,—and notwithstanding all secondary differences, there must be some general resemblance in occupation; or at least absence of such fundamental difference as that between an occupation exclusively pleasurable, and one exclusively painful.

Tension is as necessary to social vigor as to physical health. In the largest sense it may be said to be necessary to all movements, to the very movements to which it indicates restraint. Without the opposition offered by limits, the river will not run in its bed, electric currents will not traverse the wire, the sap will not mount in the tree, the blood will not circulate in the artery. So the most strenuous social movements have always been effected in a glow of heroic defiance of obstacles, all but overwhelming. The constant effort of social progress is towards the removal of obstacles, and an immense number have been removed. The question therefore arises; if progress continue in the same ratio, will not *all* obstacles finally be removed? In that case will not social effort cease, from absence of stimulus to exertion? Will not heroism be impossible when everything has become safe and easy? Will there remain any adequate employment for the activities of the largest minds and strongest characters? The herd may continue to vegetate in peace, but the heroes, the prophets, the saviours, what is to become of them?

This sense of difficulty in finding adequate occupation for the energies which crave it so imperiously, and which, if unsatisfied, suffice to desolate life, is no mere abstraction. It is rather a generalisation from the practical difficulties experienced in a great many concrete cases, precisely in the class which, as being the most distinctly articulate, is the best able to make its difficulties known.

We think an answer can best be understood after trying in imagination to project oneself for a moment to some epoch in feudal Europe, when the only recognized occupation was the art of war. It is well known that to the mailed heroes once entrenched in the high-perched castles whose ruins still dot a European landscape, the suggestion of excitement or adventure, of honor or vigorous exertion in any other employment than in that of killing something, would have seemed a childish absurdity. Art, science, literature, philosophy, industry, to-day so immense in their development, were then enfolded in their germs; or even when they had begun to make a place for themselves in the world, they were still contemptuously ignored by those who constituted its social consciousness and who make its history.

With that mediæval world, and with at least a large part of the antique world which preceded it, the modern world stands contrasted as the epoch at which the art of creating life has become prized above the art of destroying it. The opposition which quickened the pulse of the former hero of society came from the antagonism of his brother men. The opposition with which modern energy is in conflict, comes in the largest sense from the inertia of nature. Although extremely improbable, it is yet conceivable, that self-interest should one day succeed in suppressing the social manifestation of violent passions, at least sufficiently to render superfluous, armed resistance to them, and the heroism attendant on such resistance. But so far as heroism consists in courage for physical danger and for social opprobrium, in patience, perseverance and steadfast faith in the purpose conceived or received from above, so far heroism must remain a permanent element of human character, and find permanent occasion for its exercise. The difficulties of destruction are those encountered by the child; they occasion the tragedies of the nursery. The difficulties of creation stand in the way of the man,—what do we say? Are they not the eternal difficulties in the way of the gods?

In a well-known witticism, Mr. Bright is said to have called the army a system of out-door relief for the aristocracy. For centuries it has been the permanent and sufficient remedy for the ennui which otherwise must have overwhelmed the natural leaders of society, not obliged to work for their living, and not seeing their way clear to work for anything else. It is true indeed that

> "Work without hope draws water in a sieve,
> And life without an object cannot live."

But theory, based on all historical experience, the only possible basis for calculation of the future, shows that human life, personal or social, can never fail, if properly understood, to afford employment for human energies. That at present there is a most pernicious mal-distribution of energies, dependent partly on the fact that social forms and institutions have in so many cases survived the ideas in which they originated; partly on the fact, that no practical systematic attempt has yet been made to estimate the real needs of the social organism, and to distribute its forces in accordance with them. The theoretical estimate has been made by one set of people, or rather by many sets, and according to many principles. The practical direction is continued by others, and in accordance with custom, habit, tradition, temporary convenience, sentimentalism, prejudice, fashion, with everything except the principles of organic adjustment alone serviceable. Even these, when most scientifically elaborated, have too often erred, either by proposing to sacrifice the state to individual license, or individual freedom to the state, or else by adopting a systematic policy of non-intervention on the ground of a natural tendency to progress. But this last reason is as reasonable as would be the refusal of a physician to treat the diseases of dentition or of adolescence, because the patient was destined to survive, and then could not fail to grow out of the tendency to such diseases. When this individual is the social organism, its periods of suffering involve the entire sacrifice of myriads of the sentient beings, whose consciousness is the only consciousness that organism possesses.

In the feudal system which succeeded at so long an interval to the antique social organization of the city, and to the intermediate barbarian tribe, may be found the type of society upon which Comte was never weary of expatiating. A society rich, varied, flexible, yet so thoroughly harmonized by a logical and effective system of ideas that it constituted a splendid unity, whose parts were each vividly conscious of their own functions and of its splendor, and were therefore organically satisfied. An organism whose spiritual and temporal powers, unconsciously modelled upon one another, continually reinforced each other by converging all efforts and all ambitions in one direction. The hierarchy of emperor and king and lord and knight and squire, was repeated in the hierarchy of Pope and cardinal and bishop and priest and monk, and this visible spiritual hierarchy supposed to reflect so faithfully that of the invisible heavens, that these could be imagined as in close and tangible contact with the daily life of men. Then a unique prize really glittered before the eyes of all,—the hope of salvation; prize, thanks to the liberal offices of the church, attainable without much difficulty by all competitors, compelled, whatever their difference in earthly rank, to obtain the favor of heaven by the same formula of shrift and sacrament.

Thus was perfectly realized the essential condition of

an organism, namely, concurrence in a common end of the function of widely differentiated parts, which had moreover certain fundamental destinies in common. Each individual, fulfilling the special duties of his rank and station, was conscious of contributing to the maintenance of a social order established upon divine sanctions. Each in his due proportion therefore participated in the divine blessing upon earth; while each, without proportion, was supposed to look forward to an identical glory in heaven. A compact, coherent, logical society, though built for the most part on fictions, though nourished so largely by delusions, though practically ignoring the humble industrial basis upon which it was compelled to rest, but which it disdained and kept out of sight like awkward feet of clay.

The enormous transformation of modern society depends upon the prominence for the first time attained by these feet of clay, and by the retreat into relative insignificance of the head of gold, the splendid ruling classes of society. The scanty list of circumstances enumerated by Mr. Mallock as giving a "New Import" to the question of the natural or supernatural value of life, have very little to do with this question, as compared with the great social changes that really do affect it profoundly. When a society established on a purely military basis, nominally transmits its religious ideals to a society established on industrialism, and to which war has become only a disturbing incident, the most serious incongruities become inevitable; and at a distance of six centuries from the prime of feudalism, industrialism is still destitute of a logical and coherent ideal connate to itself, and is obliged to make shift with the pale recollection of that of a bye-gone state. Perhaps our modern cities stand to-day in the same place as formerly Rome and Byzantium and Alexandria, when the spirit of antiquity had fled, and mediæval society had not yet been organized; and it is possible that much of their miseries is due to this intermediate condition.

In a theological ideal which considers the world as a place unfit for anything but fighting, the aim of industrialism, to increase riches and earthly power, is entirely unprovided for, is necessarily looked upon as a "base materialism." Industrialism has therefore developed without the guidance or guardianship of any ideal; it has stumbled into power like a Caliban become blindly possessed of the secrets of Prospero. It is, as yet, scarcely conscious of itself; and the world which is yielding to it, which worships the results of its physical force, has not yet fully recognized its real soul. To-day, as in the days of Ulysses, those who aver that

> There is not a greater glory for a man while yet
> He lives on earth, than what he hath wrought out
> By strenuous effort, with his feet and hands."*

are thinking more of gymnastics than of effective industry; more of the amateur activities becoming a gentle-

---

* Odyssey, Book viii, 181–185 (Bryant's translation).

man than of the arduous labors necessary to a man. It is not yet fully recognized that labor is a physiological necessity even before it is an economic necessity. The stirring ambitions of knighthood have been forgotten, while the ancient stigma attached to unmilitary work has, singularly enough, been remembered. When this stigma has ceased to inflict political disfranchisement, it often remains as a cause of social ostracism. Or when work has been admitted to be honorable, if not unavoidable, it has been still looked upon as a hardship to be deplored. As a corollary, efforts are constantly made to secure as much profit with as little work as possible—senseless dishonesty, which vitiates the entire sum of social activities. When, however, work has been accepted with satisfaction for men, it is still almost universally withheld from women. Withheld, that is, as a normal and necessary part of a perfect life; withheld in theory, to be only more harshly and clumsily inflicted in practice; withheld from the fortunate classes in such a manner that the unfortunate classes become doubly and intolerably burdened.

The natural organic connection between the head of gold and the feet of clay has therefore been destroyed. The head reels in dizzy and aimless vacuity: the feet flounder deeper and deeper in the mire. Those who formerly led the masses to battle have ceased to do that, but have not yet learned how to lead them to work. Hence all community between the rank and the file has disappeared. The workers look with envy and hatred at those who enjoy the fruit of their labors without properly participating in them; the rich, from this same absence in participation, are unable to enjoy; the church—former reconciler of rich and poor—now stands apart, mumbling useless formulas, or chattering of imaginary dangers, as if to conceal its impotence over those which really exist.

There can be no belief without an idea and an emotion, and no emotion without action, and no disinterested emotion without action in relation to some interest transcending that of individual concerns. Religious interest has never been disinterested when limited to the care of saving one's own soul. Whenever really powerful and ennobling as a social force, it has been identified with some great sweep of social action, in which individual lives have been caught up, as it were, to meet the ideal passion in the air. The dream of heaven never has had influence except when the dreamers have been actively engaged in realizing it upon earth. Nothing can be more absurd and in more naïve contradiction of well known history than the assertion made by Mr. Mallock and others, that Positivism has *destroyed* heaven, and with it all the ideal aspirations of mankind. It is well known that for centuries the Christians looked forward daily to the establishment of heaven upon earth, and that their entire theology was originally constructed under the influence of this expectation.

As the hope receded farther and farther away, Christian feudalism first took the place of the heavenly society of which hope had been abandoned. To-day Positivism seeks to bring back the vanished dream of the early Christians; it seeks to establish heaven upon earth. This is what Mr. Mallock calls wallowing in the mire of an indiscriminate sensualism.

It is with Catholicism that Positivism must be constantly compared and contrasted, and not with Protestantism, nor with the looser systems of Free Thought which have never embodied themselves in definite social institutions. Positivism intends step by step to replace Catholicism in every detail. To substitute as far as it may, knowledge for faith, effort for passivity, the social organism of European civilization for the feudal organism of Catholic Europe, with its imagined correlative of a heavenly kingdom. Instead of a social order commanding individual effort and enthusiasm on account of external divine sanctions, Positivism declares that society is intrinsically worthy of efforts and enthusiasm. It does not change the fundamental direction of disinterested feeling: it merely removes an artificial stamp once supposed to be the source of value—as one who should remove an unnecessary certificate from solid gold. "Take away religion from those things in life we have been accustomed to prize," says Mr. Mallock, "and nothing will be left, not even pleasure in a walk on a fine day." But Positivism claims to demonstrate both by historical and by psychological evidence—that if we take away earthly passions, interests and activities from theology, nothing will remain in it but a ghostly vision, an unsubstantial dream. The charm, supposed to belong to the infinite, has largely belonged to the very definite limits within which the infinite has been confined. Since nothing can be obtained or even perceived by man except through the medium of his own faculties, whatever enlarges his faculties enlarges his horizon; whatever compresses them, narrows his sphere of thought and feeling, no less than of action.

Catholicism has measured the area of a cathedral, and called it the Infinite. Positivism, reaching out to the immeasurable sky, contemplates the unlimited. Life under Catholicism resembles a Connecticut farm, covered with stone walls, so much the more solidly built, as the fields which they enclose are the more barren. Life, in the conception of the Positivist thought, may be likened to an Illinois prairie, whose fertile acres do not yield stony material enough for the rapid building of rigid boundaries, but must await more genial decisions from the future unfettered cultivators of the soil. Catholicism is the religion of failure, of ignorance, of weakness, of despair; the essence of its power and of its attractiveness lies in the consolation it professes to offer to those who cannot get what they want. Positivism is the philosophy of strength; it undertakes to show people how to get what they want; and it is less consoling when it fails. It gives a sense of religious obligations for the utilization of powers; but affects no complacency at the spectacle of their mutilation. As one of the characteristic dangers of Catholicism is in the passive toleration of evils which it encourages while cultivating humanity and patience; so a characteristic danger of Positivism is the tendency it may foster to an impatient and arrogant selfishness of grasp, which may be promoted by insisting on the legitimacy of the satisfactions of life, and on the cruelty of their privation. But the power of self-abnegation and self-sacrifice which Catholicism derives from its promise of future compensation, Positivism derives from the consciousness of social welfare, and from the cultivated habit of subordinating immediate personal impulses to higher sentiments of justice, of honor, of sympathy. When however, the personal sacrifice demanded is an injustice; when, as at present, passionate feeling revolts at miseries entailed by the selfishness, or ignorance, or the stupidity, or the tyranny of other persons or classes; the moderation comes, not from fictitious acquiescence in evil as good; nor from fictitious submission to an arbitrary providence; nor from hope of personal escape; but from a human sympathy so wide and deep, that it prefers to bide its time, to share in a common suffering, rather than to endanger a common cause by premature impatience and personal greed. Unless this noble humanity succeed in taking the place left vacant by the loss of other motives, what is to prevent the feet of clay from one day trampling to pieces the head of gold, which had abdicated its lawful power and authority?

Thus we return to the conception of the social organism, as the only one capable of rescuing modern society from its present state of anarchy. We are far more thoroughly convinced than Mr. Mallock can be, that the acceptance of this conception as a basis, not only for social action but for individual life, can only be accomplished by means of many transformations in existing habits of thought and feeling.

It necessitates the wide distribution of a scientific understanding of life; of the laws of its development; of the complex basis of its morality; necessitates even more, a different training of feeling, which may facilitate a different estimate of values than at present generally obtains. But many of these transformations have been avowedly accomplished. Others are really effected, though the change is concealed under false names. Others would be, were it not for the still existing opposition between the beliefs which are nominally paraded as the protecting æges of society, and those which really animate even its priesthoods. It is the enthusiastic duty of all who witness lives, distracted, or blighted, or withered by the far reaching influence, either in themselves or in those who control their destinies—of beliefs contrary to the real nature of things, to promote the spread of the true principles of living.

Will no one suffer?—Has no one suffered?

It is difficult to imagine that the destinies of the race

conceal any greater sufferings than those which it has already traversed. In plagues, pestilence and famine; in battle, murder and sudden death; in envy, hatred and all uncharitableness; in all woes from which a sonorous litany may pray ineffectively for deliverance,—may be read the impotence of theology. For whatever suffering may come, we cannot but be prepared, if experience is to be relied upon to prepare us. It is our business to seek the new good of which, indeed, we have had much foretaste and keen realization, but which, in all soberness we may now begin to anticipate in much fuller measure, when each restless, passionate, eagerly active and keenly sensitive human being shall find his place and fulfil his function in the vast Living Being of Humanity. Then will literally be fulfilled the ancient prophecy, "Ye shall be as gods, knowing good and evil." It will be found that the Tree of Life grows forever by the Tree of Knowledge, and that, after its long exile, the race which has once become possessed of the fatal fruit of the one, may re-enter an earthly Paradise to enjoy the other. And we may dare to say, that if society to-day be really in the position of a man who awakes from a dream, it is certain that any temporary regrets he may feel, must ultimately be more than compensated by the full possession of the dawning realities.

APPENDIX.

In the social organism, Comte did not include the populations of Asia and Africa, but only the nations of Europe. In an embryological comparison, Europe would represent the germinal area of the fecundated ovum, we might even say the Mediteranean basin would represent the germinal spot. The course of development would be in accordance, not with the type of the ova of highest or mammalian vertebrates, but with that of the eggs of birds, reptiles and fishes. In the mammalia, the ovum is nourished by the parent organism, and the whole of its mass enters into the composition of the germ. But the mass of the ova of birds is divided between the germ and the yolk destined to nourish the germ. The social organism corresponds to this latter type. The germ, the embryo, is constituted by European civilization, gradually consolidated from elements that have been drawn from without into the germinal area ; as the blastoderm is formed from a gradual condensation of granules and globules which were originally distributed throughout the ovum, but are finally accumulated at a limited part of it. The rest of the world is divided into the colonial offshoots of this civilization, and into the subordinate civilizations or barbarisms which in various ways nourish the life of Europe, and are probably destined to be absorbed by it. Thus if Europe be the blastoderm, Asia and Africa compose the yolk of the gigantic earth ovum.